The Spiritual Power
of Nonviolence

The Spiritual Power of Nonviolence

Interfaith Understanding for a Future Without War

George W. Wolfe

**With a Foreword by Bishop William E. Swing
and
Swami Harshananda**

JOMAR Press
1002 Wisteria Trail
Austin, Texas 78753
www.JOMARPress.com

Cover design by Alfredo Marin-Carle.

Library of Congress Control Number: 2010913263
ISBN: Hardcover   978-1-4535-7290-0
                   Softcover   978-1-4535-7289-4
                   Ebook   978-1-4535-7291-7

All the images in this book are in the public domain.

This book was printed in the United States of America.

To order additional copies of this book, contact:
Xlibris Corporation
1-888-795-4274
www.Xlibris.com
Orders@Xlibris.com
71665

More endorsements for *The Spiritual Power of Nonviolence* . . .

Physical war is never "holy." George Wolfe delivers a thought-provoking call for all people of faith to search and study their scriptures, seeking to extract the higher meaning in the application of God's Word, as each of us continues the struggle for peace, justice and that which is righteous.

Imam Michael "Mikal" Saahir
Nur-Allah Islamic Center
Indianapolis, Indiana

It is high time to end this era of militarism and bring peace to our world through our wisdom mind, and applying the strategies for peace mentioned by Professor Wolfe in this book will definitely help. I truly appreciate his peace work!

Geshe Jinpa Sonam, Spiritual Director,
Indiana Buddhist Center

Professor Wolfe has delved deep into the scriptures of the world religions to get support for his thesis that war is an evil which solves no problems and peace and nonviolence are needed for the survival and progress of humanity.

N. Krishnaswamy, President
Swami Vivekananda Education Society
Bangalore, India

Other Publications by George Wolfe

*Inner Space as Sacred Space: The Temple
as Metaphor for the Mystical Experience*

Common Themes in the World's Great Religions

Parallel Teachings in Hinduism and Christianity

In the Shadow of the Sun: A Portrait of India

The Master Remembered

His words were the alchemist's gold, strung on a
  thread connecting minds and mesons.*
When he spoke, the vacuum trembled, for a
  moment unveiling the timeless.

Arrowed pines split the moonlight as he sat in
  quantum stillness,
Listening between thoughts to the One applauding
  itself.†

"Revelation," he explained, "is a seed without a
  cause, an impulse by which the universe sings.
Anticipate its appearance, and it will elude you."

Then I perceived as one imprisoned by atoms.
Now his words are collisions within the silence
  through which the light-years pass.

GW

---

*   A class of subatomic particles that participate in both weak and strong interactions.

†   An allusion to the Zen koan: "What is the sound of one hand clapping?" Because God
    is beyond duality, God only has one hand to clap with.

Contents

Foreword

I

If you could imagine the enjoyment of sitting down with a widely read person who has an amazing ability to make connections among disparate thinkers, someone with a clear and strong conviction about violence, then you are in for a treat. That is who George Wolfe is, and that is what he has done in his book *The Spiritual Power of Nonviolence: Interfaith Understanding for a Future Without War.* And his message is sometimes very personal.

I spend my days working to end religiously motivated violence, and I carry around with me a solid Christian theological education, plus a scattering of knowledge of other faiths and worldviews. What I find hard is to "connect the dots." That is not difficult for Professor Wolfe. The phoenix myth, Jesus' resurrection, and the teachings of Buckminster Fuller are all telling the same story, according to Wolfe. His book is one of strange bedfellows.

This is not a book in which the reader wonders about the point of the story. From the beginning, George Wolfe exposes his hand. For him, violence with a good end in mind is a very bad idea. There are other paths, regenerative and muscular paths, that can take civilization on a much healthier journey. With a sense of urgency, he points to those paths. In a world that quickly ratchets up hostilities and hastily entertains wars and suicide strategies for success, his book presents an important option for the reader.

The Rt. Rev. William E. Swing
Episcopal bishop of California (retired)
President and founder,
United Religions Initiative

II

"Ahimsa is the highest virtue"—declare the Hindu scriptures. Ahimsa or nonviolence is a necessary condition for a peaceful life, but not sufficient. It is universal love, a deep respect for life that actually supplements it and fulfills it.

The world has seen enough wars, the ugly ones and the uglier ones. The ugliest one is just round the corner if nuclear madness gets the better of human wisdom, a little of which still seems to exist.

If wars are born in the minds of men, so is peace. The basis for peace lies in the deep-rooted conviction about the power of goodness. Goodness and love are concomitant; nonviolence is the starting point for both.

In this book entitled *The Spiritual Power of Nonviolence: Interfaith Understanding for a Future Without War*, Professor George Wolfe of the Center for Peace and Conflict Studies at Ball State University has argued his case very effectively, carrying us through seven well-written chapters, each imbued with proof material and also spiritual conviction.

Any right-thinking person who goes through this script should feel that much more convinced about the spiritual power of nonviolence and place one more brick on the foundation of world peace through his heartfelt prayer for a violence-free world.

Swami Harshananda
President
Ramakrishna Math,
Bangalore-560019, India

Author's Note

This book examines religion, war, and theories relevant to nonviolence from an interfaith perspective. I have therefore chosen the designations CE (Common Era) and BCE (Before the Common Era) as a substitute for the traditional Western labels BC (Before Christ) and AD (Anno Domini).

Unless otherwise indicated, all biblical references are from the Revised Standard Version and checked against the *Alfred Marshall Interlinear Greek-English New Testament* (Grand Rapids: Zondervan Publishing House, 1975). Some Bible verses have been edited to favor the use of inclusive language. Passages from the Qur'an, unless noted otherwise, are from *The Meaning of the Holy Qur'an* by Abdullah Yusuf Ali.

Acknowledgments

It takes a village to write a book. That is what I soon discovered after embarking on this literary project. I am sincerely grateful to all my colleagues who took time to read and critique earlier versions of the manuscript as I prepared it for publication.

Special thanks must go to Rev. James Wolfe. As a world religions professor, his recommendations were invaluable as I developed and solidified my interfaith theology. Susan Tellman also deserves special commendation. A former creative writing professor, she is a brilliant writer herself. Her suggestions made a huge difference in the quality of my literary style.

Father Keith Hosey, Sister Maureen Mangan, Rev. David Cartwright, Rev. Thomas Perchlik, Dr. Bryce E. Taylor, Dr. Lynn Sousa, Dr. Jody Nagel, Mr. Jon Schuck, and Dr. Larry Gerstein helped critique specific sections of the manuscript according to their expertise. I am particularly thankful to Bishop William E. Swing, Mr. Arun Gandhi, Rabbi Raine Teller, Dr. Michael N. Nagler, Swami Harshananda, Judy O'Bannon, Imam Michael "Mikel" Saahir, Geshe Jinpa Sonam, and Dr. N. Krishnaswamy for the time they took, not only to read the text but also to write endorsements that helped launch its publication. In addition, Dr. Melkote Shivaswamy, Mr. Paul Stout, Dr. Yeno Matuka, my daughter Esther Wolfe, and my wife Susan Magrath meticulously read and corrected this manuscript at different stages in its development.

Finally, I must thank Roger McConnell, director of America's Hometown Band, for letting me stay at his lakeside lodge so I could write without distractions, and Alfredo Marin-Carle, an exceptionally gifted graphic artist in the Ball State University Department of Journalism, for designing the cover art.

Introduction

The last days of April 1992 were tumultuous for the state of California. An earthquake measuring 7.2 on the Richter scale shook Cape Mendocino in Humboldt County on April 25th. Four days later on April 29th, rioting erupted in Los Angeles after a predominately white jury acquitted four police officers in the beating of Rodney King, a black motorist who had led police on a high-speed chase. Property damage in LA surpassed $1 billion. Thousands were injured and over 50 people died. Both the human toll and the material cost of the violence in Los Angeles greatly exceeded the damage done by the natural disaster in Humboldt County.

I was living in Marin County north of San Francisco at the time. Around 4 PM, I turned on the television expecting to hear news of the violent protest. What I saw, however, was another form of protest, one being conducted with the kind of civil restraint and discipline that was exemplified by the nonviolent activism of Mahatma Gandhi and Martin Luther King Jr.

Demonstrators had assembled on the Oakland Bay Bridge in the middle of rush hour. In groups of six, they sat in the middle of the highway, blocking the flow of traffic. Once seated, the activists were arrested and ushered away by police, only to be replaced by another half-dozen activists. The protest continued for more than two hours.

Compared to the violent uprisings in the streets of Los Angeles, the demonstration on the Oakland Bay Bridge made a powerful public statement without causing harm to property or human life. It captivated the media that afternoon like demonstrations are intended to do. Because it was conducted as a peaceful protest with restraint and self-control, news reporters could easily cover the event without placing themselves in danger. Many of those responsible for the violence in Los Angeles were charged with felonies and would spend years in prison. Those arrested on the Oakland Bay Bridge were soon released and thereby could continue their activism.

Watching the reports of these protests on television led me to ponder two pressing questions. How can we convince people the world over to renounce violence and use only honorable, nonviolent strategies to express their anger toward what they perceive as unjust? What role should religion be playing in today's world to make it possible for our children to inherit a future without war?

The Good Samaritan as Activist

Each of the most prominent world religions embraces some form of the golden rule. The ancient Indian epic, the *Mahabharata*, states it as follows: "This is the sum of duty: Do not do to others what you would not have them do unto you."[1] The Buddhist rendition is similar: "Treat not others in ways you yourself would find hurtful."[2] In the Talmud, Rabbi Hillel is credited with stating the golden rule as the essence of the Torah: "What is hateful to yourself, do not do to your fellow man. That is the whole Torah; the rest is commentary."[3] The Gospel of Matthew quotes Jesus as presenting it in a positive form: "So whatever you wish that others would do to you, do so to them, for this is the Law and the prophets."[4]

Why would Matthew's gospel restate Rabbi Hillel in the positive? Perhaps it is because someone could misinterpret the negative form of the golden rule as allowing a person to be complacent or to refrain from acting. The well-known parable of the Good Samaritan addresses this concern when interpreted from the perspective of social activism. In the parable, a priest and a Levite* pass by a Jew lying in the road who had been beaten, robbed, and left for dead. They choose not to become involved, perhaps for religious reasons, so as not to be defiled by a corpse. Then a Samaritan approaches and, seeing the man, acts to help the victim.[5] Action is necessary if we hope to make the world a better place.

The priest and the Levite did not violate the "letter" of Rabbi Hillel's version of the golden rule when passing by the man on the road, particularly if they believed he was dead. They did nothing that was hateful. Expressing the golden rule in the positive, however (i.e., *do* unto others), at least requires that a person investigate what happened to see if something can be done.

Jesus taught this parable when a lawyer, after reciting the Great Commandments to love God and to love your neighbor as yourself, asked,

---

*   Levite: a member of the Hebrew tribe of Levi who assisted the priests in the Jewish temples.

"And who is my neighbor?"[6] At the time, Samaritans were a segment of the Jewish population who, over many years, had grown apart from the Jews in Jerusalem. The two groups despised each other, mostly on religious grounds.* Theologian James D. Purvis refers to their separation as a schism and describes their relationship as hostile.[7] The parable of the Good Samaritan was thus a challenge to the Jerusalem Jewish elite, but it also contains a message of how to initiate reconciliation that is often overlooked. For the Samaritan sets aside his hatred and reaches out to assist an adversary who is in need. He even plans to return a few days later to be sure the man he rescued was properly cared for.

It is challenging to place the Good Samaritan parable in other cultures using different conflicting ethnic groups. Rather than involving characters that represent the Jewish leaders in Jerusalem and the Samaritans, have them be Tibetans and the Han Chinese, Israelis and Palestinians, or Protestants and Catholics in Northern Ireland. The parable makes a strong statement for placing our common humanity over our individual or collective grievances, and asks us to reach outside the strict adherence to religious law.

From Seville to Flight 90

The golden rule is a simple teaching, perhaps too simple to overcome our human capacity for fear, jealousy, anger, and the desire for revenge. While popular religion appeals to our ideals and altruistic sensibilities, it has a poor historical record when it comes to stopping violence. Whether in their cultural development or in their scriptures, the religions of the world all have been guilty at times of condoning, even endorsing, violence and war. Their tainted history has caused many people today to forsake organized religion in favor of a more personal expression of nonaligned spirituality.

Some evolution theorists have maintained the reason for war is that violence is in our genes. Because humans evolved from a lower primate, we have inherited aggressive defense and survival mechanisms that enabled us to successfully compete as hunter-gatherers in the pre-civilized world. These aggressive traits influence human behavior, causing us to have a predisposition for violence. Referred to as biological determinism, this view asserts that war is inevitable and intrinsic to the human condition.[8]

---

* Among their differences, the Samaritans had their own version of the Pentateuch (the five books of Moses) and worshipped on Mt. Gerizim rather than on Mt. Zion.

According to the United Nations Educational, Scientific and Cultural Organization (UNESCO), studies in the 1980s revealed this notion was prevalent, with roughly 50 percent of the people surveyed believing that humans are predisposed to war and violence.[9]

In response, leading behavioral scientists representing twelve nations produced *The Seville Statement on Violence*, which was published in 1991. This document refuted the dangerously simplistic generalizations of biological determinism. While primates, including humans, do possess aggressive traits, they also exhibit cooperative and altruistic behaviors. It is incorrect to assume that aggressive traits have been selected through evolution more so than other kinds of behaviors. The scientists concluded "that biology does not condemn humanity to war, and that humanity can be freed from the bondage of biological pessimism."[10]

On January 13, 1982, an unassuming man demonstrated a level of altruistic behavior that defies the popular view that survival was the underlying determinate in human evolution. Arland Williams was a passenger on Air Florida flight 90. Soon after takeoff, the airliner lost altitude and crashed in Washington DC, hitting the Fourteenth Street bridge before plunging into the icy waters of the Potomac River. Williams, along with five other passengers to survive the crash, were spotted in the river in desperate need of help. A police helicopter arrived and dropped a rescue line. Arland Williams grabbed the line and handed it to one of the flight attendants. He did this a second time, and perhaps a third time as well. When the helicopter returned a final time, Williams had disappeared under the frigid waters.[11] The following year, President Reagan honored Williams, posthumously awarding him the United States Coast Guard's Gold Lifesaving Medal.

The actions of Arland Williams on that bitter January day reveal the altruistic side of human nature, one that is inherently self-sacrificing, compassionate, and responsive to the needs of others. This selfless and heroic human potential, when awakened on moral grounds in large numbers of people, is what makes successful nonviolence possible.

Thinking Outside the Tomb

After returning from my first trip to India in 1992, I gave several presentations at local churches. The focus of my talks consisted of the many similar themes, symbols, and stories that I had discovered when comparing Christian and Hindu scriptures. Many of these symbols are metaphors for what in Indian philosophy and Buddhism is referred to as self-realization or enlightenment. I was soon led to the Gnostic writings that include the Gospel of Thomas. This investigation added credence to my personal view that Jesus intended his teaching to be a means of awakening the spirit within. Through this awakening, the "secrets of the kingdom of heaven,"[12] as expressed in parables and myths, are revealed to the earnest seeker.

Jesus' message was intended for everyone regardless of class, education, culture, or ethnicity. He ate with tax collectors and sinners, spoke to the Samaritan woman at the well, forgave the adulteress, and healed lepers and people suffering from mental illness.* When Jesus healed the Roman ruler's daughter and the woman who had been hemorrhaging for twelve years, they expressed their faith through trust and surrender.[13] Jesus did not require a prescribed confession of belief.

This inclusive spirit, however, soon became a casualty of church politics. By 200 CE, the diversity of religious belief and practice among early Christians was being suppressed. Irenaeus and other bishops of this period declared Gnosticism a heresy, and an effort to formulate a unifying church doctrine was underway.[14]

The first Christian emperor was Constantine the Great, who ruled the eastern part of a divided Roman empire. He and Licinius, his co-emperor who presided over the western empire, issued a short-lived proclamation of religious tolerance in 313 CE. Known as the Edict of Milan, it temporarily ended the persecution of Christians. But Licinius reneged on the agreement. The rivalry between Constantine and Licinius eventually culminated in a religious civil war from which Constantine emerged victorious.[15]

In 325 CE, with Constantine as the sole emperor, the first Council of Nicaea was convened. Subsequently, the council's influence over the church became a divisive force, deciding what books should comprise the New Testament and insisting Christians accept the doctrine of the Trinity as professed in the Nicene Creed. A priest named Arius, who served congregations in Alexandria, challenged the Trinity concept, but he and his followers were overwhelmingly voted down at Nicaea. After Constantine's reign, in 367 CE, the archbishop of Alexandria, Athanasius, ordered books containing heretical ideas destroyed.[16] Reliance on dogma as a defense against

---

* From biblical times until the late 1800s, people with mental illness were thought to be possessed by demons. Stories of Jesus casting out demons are best understood as instances where he healed someone suffering from a form of mental illness.

heresy was increasingly emphasized over reliance on personal insight. It became more and more difficult to follow one's light within.

In my church presentations, I would quote the familiar gospel passage where Jesus tells his followers to let their light shine forth and not hide it under a bushel.[17] I then would point out the following irony. The church, by imposing a rigid dogma, denying possible influences from Eastern sources, and repressing the theological insights of mystics, was shrouding the light of Christ. As the church evolved over the centuries, it had, in fact, become the bushel.

This is not to say that we should automatically reject religious dogma. Every religion has its prescribed beliefs. Dogma can be useful in helping a person question and think more deeply. What is at fault here is not so much the dogma but a priestly hierarchy insisting on rigid acquiescence to doctrine.*

My study of non-Christian writings did not stop with Hindu scripture. I soon began exploring Taoist, Buddhist, Native American, and Islamic writings as well. The result was the evolution of a unique cross-cultural perspective that, along with my involvement in peace studies, crystallized as a nonviolent interfaith theology. It is a theology that is particularly timely as the nations of the world are forced to grapple with religious pluralism.

Embracing an interfaith theology, however, requires that we think outside the confines of dogma and accepted conventions, much like we are challenged to do in Zen Buddhist philosophy. I tell my fellow Christians they need to "think outside the tomb."

Each of the world religions has contributed to what I call the collective wisdom of humanity. It is our duty as educated citizens to appreciate the contribution each religion has made to the ethical and philosophical teachings that comprise this collective wisdom. Whenever we try to define God, we metaphorically place God in a tomb. When we return three days later, God will no longer be there. The tomb we have constructed will be empty. Our conceptual framework, no matter how insightful, cannot contain the infinite

---

*   Early church dogma often originated as a defense against a belief that was deemed heretical. Christian contemplatives, however, have been known to approach dogma creatively, extracting positive meaning. For mystics, the Holy Spirit is experienced as the intense flow of love between the Creator and the creation as symbolized by the love between a father and his son. The Spirit of God then is perceived as the movement of love and compassion at work in creation.

creative power and life-source we refer to as God. Yet, it is in experiencing emptiness that we are provoked into searching for deeper meaning.

As I was documenting the similar teachings found in the scriptures of the world religions, an organization was born in California whose mission was to end religiously motivated violence. The Rt. Rev. William E. Swing, now-retired Episcopal bishop of California, envisioned an organization that would function in a way comparable to the United Nations, only seeking to foster better understanding among the great faith traditions while mediating conflicts between religious groups around the world.

After meeting with religious and government leaders in various countries, Bishop Swing formed the organization known as the United Religions Initiative. Several other interfaith organizations have since emerged with similar missions, mostly in the United States (see appendix 1). This book is designed to contribute to the fields of religion and peace studies, explaining how nonviolence can be applied to promote reform, forgiveness, and reconciliation in societies where injustice and religious differences generate hostility in the social landscape.

The Dangerous Professor

In the fall of 2004, the U.S.-led war in Iraq was in its second year. National right-wing political commentator David Horowitz began criticizing collegiate peace studies programs throughout the country, claiming they were indoctrinating students with a liberal anti-American political agenda. As director of the Center for Peace and Conflict Studies at Ball State University, I became one of his prime targets, along with peace studies faculty teaching in Indiana at Earlham College and Purdue University. Mr. Horowitz used his Internet publication *Frontpage Magazine*, as well as conservative radio and television talk shows, to launch his nationwide campaign. The Associated Press covered the controversy, and articles were run in media outlets throughout the country, including the CNN website and in *USA Today.* There is a bit of irony in the fact that the CNN and *USA Today* articles appeared during the Christmas season when Christians celebrate the birth of the Prince of Peace.

The barrage of publicity made several false and misleading statements about the peace studies program at Ball State. It even went so far as to accuse the Ball State peace center, the Muslim Students Association, and a student organization named Peaceworkers of supporting terrorism. Journalist Thomas Ryan, in his *Frontpage Magazine* article "Recruiting for Terror at

Ball State," wrote that peace studies programs were "indoctrinating students and recruiting them to agendas that are anti-American, anti-military, and friendly to the terrorist enemies intent on destroying us."[18] The Horowitz propaganda machine published a cartoon caricature depicting me playing the saxophone while the World Trade Center burned in the background. There was also an attempt by a Republican state senator to introduce a so-called Academic Bill of Rights into the Indiana House of Representatives, legislation which could have allowed politicians to oversee university course offerings and course content.

The false and misleading accusations, however, backfired on Mr. Horowitz. Two students in my class wrote a letter refuting the accusations made against me. After I submitted documentation proving the accusations were not true, Ball State University president Jo Ann Gora published a guest editorial supporting my teaching and validating the academic discipline of peace studies.[19] Soon thereafter, the Fort Wayne *Journal Gazette* and *The Star Press* of Muncie published editorials condemning Mr. Horowitz and calling for the Indiana State legislature to withdraw the Academic Bill of Rights.[20] A year later, Mr. Horowitz published his book *The Professors: The 101 Most Dangerous Academics in America*, which placed my name on a list with such authors as Howard Zinn, Juan Cole, and Noam Chomsky. Much of the chapter profiling me restated the false accusations made a year earlier despite evidence to the contrary submitted to Mr. Horowitz's organization by Ball State University provost Beverly Pitts.*

Former Ball State University student David Swindle, who now works as an editor and writer for David Horowitz, investigated the political attack on the Ball State Peace Studies program for his senior thesis. When interviewed for an article published on *Frontpage Magazine*, Mr. Swindle said,

> After months of research and 90 pages of argumentation I had come to the conclusion that George [Wolfe] had been slandered—a position I still hold passionately. None of the student's charges stood up to the facts.[21]

---

*   For a thorough discussion on the 2004-2005 political attack, see Swindle, D. ed., *Peace Studies, Academic Freedom, and Indoctrination: A Dialogue Between David Horowitz and Professor George Wolfe* (www.bsu.edu/libraries/virtualpress/wolfe/dialogue.htm).

The hate mail I received during the wave of distorted publicity from 2004 to 2007 revealed that there is a great need for professors to explain the discipline of peace studies to religious leaders, educators, politicians, and the general public. My inclusion in Mr. Horowitz's book provided me with numerous opportunities to do just that, as I began giving peace studies presentations nationally and internationally. These included lectures at Limburg Catholic University in Hasselt, Belgium, and peace-education workshops to school administrators on the Caribbean island of St. Lucia by invitation of the Ministry of Education. Such invitations are examples of what theologian Walter Wink* calls the "enemy's gift," which are the favorable opportunities a conflict provides if a person is able to subdue anger and view the dispute in a positive framework.[22] The chapters in this book evolved from several of my presentations, one of which was my keynote address at the 2008 Midwest Peace and Justice Summit. Others were lectures delivered at Chautauqua Institution in New York, Indiana University, Earlham College, the Unity Church for Creative Living near Jacksonville, Florida, and at Unitarian Universalist churches in Muncie, Indiana, and in Austin, Texas.

We can have a future, not without conflict, but without war. To create such a world, we must have a sustained movement to develop and promote peace education in school curricula, community centers, and religious organizations throughout the world. Such a movement, though not unified, is already underway. This book is one of many written to further that effort.

Time and again, humanity has set itself back decades by engaging in ruthless wars. We must not continue to let war be humanity's legacy. Let us devote ourselves to the study and application of nonviolence and build an interfaith culture of peace in the twenty-first century.

February 4, 2010
Raccoon Lakeside Lodge
Rockville, Indiana

---

* Walter Wink (b. 1935) is professor emeritus of biblical interpretation at Auburn Theological Seminary in New York City.

The nonviolent resister must often express his protest through non-cooperation or boycotts, but he realizes that these are not ends themselves; they are merely means to awaken a sense of moral shame in the opponent. The end is redemption and reconciliation. The aftermath of nonviolence is the creation of the beloved community, while the aftermath of violence is tragic bitterness.

—Rev. Dr. Martin Luther King Jr.

Chapter 1

Apocalypse Does Not Mean War

It is only the mystic who brings creativity to religion.
—Carl Jung

One of the most recognized religious images of the end-times is found in the Gospel of Matthew where Christ is portrayed as "coming on the clouds of heaven with power and great glory" at a time when "all the tribes of the earth will mourn."[1] The verse certainly suggests that the world will know when Judgment Day arrives. The apostle Paul elaborates on this image in his first epistle to the Thessalonians:

> For the Lord Himself will descend from heaven with a cry of command, with the archangels call, and with the sound of the trumpet of God, and the dead in Christ will be raised first, then we who are alive, who are left shall be caught up together in the clouds to meet the Lord in the air.[2]

The righteous being raised to meet Christ in the air at the time of the apocalypse has become known as the rapture. It is a prophecy that is vividly depicted in Michelangelo's stunning fresco on the wall behind the altar of the Sistine Chapel (figure 1). Ironically, the word *rapture* does not appear in Christian scripture. Nevertheless, it has become part of the evangelical Christian vocabulary. Matthew's gospel further describes the end of the age as when "the sun will be darkened, and the moon will not give its light, and the stars will fall from heaven, and the powers of heaven will be shaken."[3]

17

Similar to these Christian images are the events of Judgment Day as described in the Muslim Qur'an:

> What you are promised will surely take place. That is when the stars are extinguished and when the sky is split open, and when the mountains are pulverized and when the envoys are appointed their time. To what days are these deferred? To the day of judgment.[4]

Figure 1
A black-and-white image of the *Last Judgment* and rapture as depicted by Michelangelo in the Vatican Sistine Chapel.

A variation of this image is found in Michael Sells' English rendering of the Qur'an, verses 1-4 of surah 82:

> When the sky is torn
> When the Stars are scattered
> When the seas are poured forth
> When the tombs are burst open.[5]

Anyone who endorses the worldview of modern science will find it impossible to accept a literal interpretation of such passages. We know now that beyond the sky is quite the opposite of heaven. Rather than a beatific realm of Elysian Fields, there exists a hostile void—the vacuum of space. The stars, once thought to be stationary in the heavens, actually are moving away from us at tremendous speed. Shining light-years away, they could never literally "fall from heaven" as the Gospel of Matthew predicts.* Yet, prior to 1500 CE, the worldview that inspired the apocalyptic verses in the Qur'an and the canonized Christian gospels was the dominant creation paradigm.

A woodcut believed to be from the early sixteenth-century aptly illustrates this obsolete worldview (figure 2). It depicts the sky suspended over the earth like a canopy. The stars have been placed on the canopy while the sun and moon are displayed as if moving through the sky. To the lower left of the woodcut, a man peeks through the canopy to behold the many cogs and wheels that run the machinery of creation. Except for the flat earth and the obvious artistic embellishments, the image reminds us of the geocentric cosmology devised by Ptolemy (ca. 90-168 CE) and earlier Greek theorists.

To people in the Middle Ages, the idea that the sky could split open and the stars fall from heaven was surely a frightening possibility. The age of science and the discoveries that would lead humanity out of the Dark Ages into the Renaissance and the Enlightenment had yet to dawn. We must not forget that the scriptures of the world religions were written well before Magellan circumnavigated the globe, before Copernicus and Galileo

---

*   In addition to being a light or a sign in the heavens, the word *star* in ancient times served
     as a metaphor for an external guide, such as a book, prophesy, or teacher. The stars "falling
     from heaven" may actually refer to a time in human history when there will be no more
     outer lights or external guides, leaving a person only to follow the spiritual light within.
     Similarly, the tearing or splitting of the sky in the Qur'an is more appropriately understood
     as a metaphor for a powerful awakening that all people will experience simultaneously.

demonstrated how the sun's apparent movement through the sky was an illusion, and before Charles Darwin conceived his theory of evolution. The ancient prophets lived centuries before Albert Einstein theorized how time could speed up and slow down, and before Edwin Hubble discovered the universe was expanding. In contrast to our modern-day understanding of the universe, the prophets of old believed in what is now an obsolete worldview and ascribed miraculous cataclysmic events to the end of time.

In addition to being cataclysmic, apocalyptic scriptures are filled with martial images and bellicose symbols. In Hinduism, for example, the future messiah figure is Kalki, whom believers take to be the tenth and final incarnation of Vishnu, the deity of preservation. According to D. V. Singh, Kalki is to come at the end of the present age "when moral excellence would no longer exist, the rule of law would disappear, and all would be darkness." Kalki's divine mission is to "save mankind and re-establish dharma or righteousness" and "usher in a golden age, a new era of purity and peace." He is sometimes described as "riding a white horse . . . blazing like a comet" and "holding a flaming sword."[6]

Figure 2
A sixteenth-century woodcut illustrating what is now an
obsolete worldview

The return of Christ is described in the book of Revelation using a remarkably similar image:

> Then I saw the heaven open, and behold a white horse! He who sat upon it is called faithful and true, and in righteousness he judges and makes war. His eyes are like a flame of fire . . . from his mouth issues a sharp sword with which to smite the nations, and he will rule them with a rod of iron.[7]

The sword is a common cross-cultural symbol for that which separates good from evil and truth from falsehood. That it proceeds from the mouth of the Christ figure in the above quotation suggests that it is the speech of the messiah, as opposed to a literal material sword, that will be endowed with this power.*

Martial images such as these date back at least six hundred years before the advent of Christianity to Persia where lived the prophet Zoroaster. Also known by his Greek name Zarathustra, Zoroaster taught a dualistic philosophy. The world, he said, was created by two forces, that of good called Ahura Mazda and that of evil known as Angra Mainyu. It was as if the earth serves as the battleground in the war between these powerful forces as the god of good needed humans to help him conquer evil.[8] Such dualism was also found in Greek Gnosticism and in Jewish Essene theology, where the forces of light and darkness were seen as influencing human behavior in this terrestrial world.[9] Zoroaster taught that if we use evil against evil, we merely add to the evil. We play into the hands of the enemy, allowing evil to delude us into believing we are justified in committing evil in the name of good. He therefore concluded that we must strive to overcome evil with good and prescribed the simple threefold teaching: "good thoughts, good words and good deeds."[10]

The dualistic view of good versus evil and light versus darkness also found its way into Christian scripture as evident in the following passage from the Gospel of John: "The light has come into the world, and men loved darkness rather than the light, because their deeds were evil, for anyone who does evil hates the light."[11]

It is no coincidence that many leaders of nonviolent movements—Mahatma Gandhi, Martin Luther King Jr., Cesar Chavez, Archbishop Desmond Tutu,

---

* The sword is also a prominent symbol in the Sikh religion.

and the current Dalai Lama—have also served as spiritual leaders. Social justice issues have the power to attract and unite people of diverse cultural and spiritual backgrounds. I want to make a distinction, however, between spirituality and religion because religion has a dark side that needs to be addressed. While the Spirit can bring people together, inspire them to speak out against injustice and call for social, political, and economic reforms, religion tends to divide humanity and has been used to justify violence and reinforce class divisions.

Misguided faith convincing us that committing evil is justified in the name of good reinforces the belief that violence can play a redemptive role in an individual's life or in the religious identity of a nation. In monotheistic cultures, religiously motivated political leaders have used violence to impose an order thought to be sanctioned by God. Violence comes to serve a sacrificial purpose and is believed to free a person or a nation from evil or fulfill a sacred prophecy.

Tragically, the great religions of the world—particularly Judaism, Christianity, and Islam—have, at some time in their recorded history, engaged in violence under this delusion. Some definitive examples include (1) the ancient Israelites believing God commanded them to make war as they entered the land of Canaan, which they claimed was their Promised Land;[12] (2) the Christian Crusades, the battle cry for which was "God wills it"; (3) present-day jihadists in fundamentalist Islam; and (4) fundamentalist Christians who support Middle East conflicts out of the belief they are a necessary prelude to the return of Christ. This is not to say that all expressions of redemptive violence are the same. The common underlying characteristic of religiously motivated violence, however, is the belief that God has sanctioned its use. It is rooted in a highly destructive ideology that sows the seeds for future animosity and violent conflict.

The deadly effect of religiously motivated violence is exhibited in modern-day terrorism. Politicians and commentators now recognize that confronting such ideological motivation requires innovative strategies. Conservative columnist George Will, for example, has proposed that cooperation between intelligence gathering and law enforcement should be emphasized over military intervention.[13] In addition, peace-building diplomacy and incentives that appeal to moderate factions within the religious traditions involved in the conflict must give mainstream moderate voices ample opportunity to be heard.

An Inner Struggle

Apocalyptic rhetoric by politicians and clergy appears to be inspired by religious texts and doctrines, the belief in an obsolete worldview, and a literal interpretation of the end-times. Years before the first Iraq war, televangelist James Robinson maintained that it was "heresy" and against God's Word to teach that peace will come before Christ's return.[14] During his term as president of the United States, George Herbert Walker Bush referred to Saddam Hussein as a "lawless" man, which is how the apostle Paul describes the Antichrist.[15] The president further spoke of the restructuring of Eastern Europe after the collapse of the Soviet Union as an emerging "new world order," a popular apocalyptic phrase used by Christian evangelicals.[16]

The reverend Jerry Falwell, when speaking of terrorists in an interview on CNN, said the United States should "blow them away in the name of the Lord."[17] In several of his speeches, Mahmoud Ahmadinejad, the current president of Iran, has spoken of the imminent return of the Twelfth Imam, an Islamic messiah figure who, he claims, will reestablish the nation of Islam, bringing to the world justice and peace.[18] Ahmadinejad has also called for the destruction of Israel, predicting that nations supporting Israel will be consumed in the "fire" of the Islamic nation's fury.*

With this rhetoric and the misguided beliefs that support it, there is great risk that the violent interpretation of the apocalypse will become a self-fulfilling prophecy, even to the point of believing a nuclear exchange is inevitable. It is a prophecy rooted in an antiquated fundamentalist worldview that ignores reason and the discoveries of science. To counter this millennium madness, we must articulate an alternative nonviolent view of apocalypse that explains how apocalyptic images need not be interpreted as literal to be fulfilled.

Among believers, there are those called mystics who seek to know God through direct experience rather than through outward signs or the written word. This experience is considered ineffable. All scriptures—be they the Bible, the Qur'an, the Vedas, the Dhammapada, or the Tao Te Ching—are viewed as pale reflections of the Ultimate Reality.[19] Divine wisdom is that which illumines one's spiritual path along an inward journey of personal growth toward spiritual enlightenment. The prophecies, histories, and

---

*   For more discussion on the religious language being used by world leaders, see "Iran, Bush and the Second Coming" at www.perrspectives.com/blog/archives/000376.htm

parables found in the great world religious traditions are then to be understood for their allegorical, symbolic meaning.

The Christian scriptures contain many significant examples of the benevolent use of martial symbols that are clearly intended to serve as metaphors for inner moral struggles as opposed to outer military engagements. The apostle Paul, in the thirteenth chapter of his letter to the church in Rome, calls upon his followers to "cast off the works of darkness and put on the armor of light."[20] He also characterizes his spiritual journey as an inner struggle or "war" between the "law of sin which dwells in my members" and the "law of God, in my inmost self."[21] The final chapter of the letter to the Ephesians makes ample use of martial symbols as the author calls upon his followers to wage this inner battle:

> Stand, therefore, having girded your loins with truth, and having put on the breastplate of righteousness, and having shod your feet with the equipment of the gospel of peace; above all taking the shield of faith, with which you can quench all the flaming darts of the evil one. And take the helmet of salvation, and the sword of the Spirit, which is the Word of God.[22]

Success in this inner battle enables a person to observe Jesus' teaching, "Love your enemies and do good to those who hate you,"[23] and honor the benevolent words of the apostle Paul who, like Zoroaster, taught, "Do not overcome evil with evil, but overcome evil with good."[24] In the Gospel of Matthew, Jesus is quoted as saying, "The kingdom of heaven has suffered violence, and men of violence take it by force."[25] Now, instead of imposing his heavenly kingdom through violence, Christ is portrayed as offering himself as a sacrifice to hatred and violence. He demonstrates through his life and death that his message is intended to be the antithesis of redemptive violence and ultimately, to put an end to it.

In the West, the Arabic word *jihad* is commonly thought to refer to a holy war. In Islam, however, it actually means "struggle." In fact, the phrase "holy war" does not occur in the Qur'an. Militant Islamic extremists have hijacked the word jihad much like the Ku Klux Klan in America hijacked the Christian cross when they set it ablaze to terrorize minorities. Numerous scholars explain that the primary meaning of jihad connotes an inner struggle "against one's own disobedient and ungodly inclinations,"[26] and moderate

Muslims denounce its association with terrorism. Islamic commentator Faiz Rahman states it concisely as follows:

> The literal meaning of the Arabic word "jihad" . . . is struggle . . . First and foremost, it can be an internal and personal struggle against temptation. Secondly, it can be a struggle to eradicate injustice from a society. Thirdly, it can be an armed struggle against aggression . . . Conversely, terrorism . . . is stealthily committed by persons or groups to intimidate civilians, and it has no moral bindings . . . There is absolutely no connection between jihad and terrorism, even though some terrorists claim they are doing jihad . . . They represent neither Islam nor the vast majority of Muslims who adhere to Islam.[27]

It is apparent in the Qur'an that the enemies of the faith are either those who reject monotheism or who are believers but live a life of hypocrisy. Devout Christians and Jews who follow Abrahamic monotheism are to be accepted. As comparative religion scholar Karen Armstrong emphasizes in her book *The Battle for God*, the Qur'an "recognizes the validity of all rightly guided religion, and praises all the great prophets of the past."[28]

Few people in the West are aware of the following inclusive verse in the Qur'an that appears to endorse the peaceful coexistence of Muslims, Jews, and Christians:

> Those who believe (in the Qur'an), and those who follow the Jewish (scriptures), and the Christians and the Sabians—any who believe in Allah and the Last Day, and work righteousness, shall have their reward with their Lord; on them shall be no fear, nor shall they grieve.[29]

In addition, recent archeological evidence suggests that Christians and Muslims may have shared the same pilgrimage site and prayed within the same structure when venerating Mary, the mother of Jesus.[30]

Nevertheless, the Qur'an and the Bible do contain verses in which devotees are called upon to slay those people judged as enemies. Consider, for example, the following passages from the books of Numbers and Deuteronomy:

Now therefore, kill every male among the little ones, and kill
every woman who has known man by lying with him. But all the
young girls who have not known man by lying with him, keep
alive for yourselves.[31]

When the Lord your God has given them over to you, and you
defeat them, then you must utterly destroy them; you shall make
no covenant with them, and show no mercy to them.[32]

And from the Qur'an

Remember thy Lord inspired the angels (with the message): "I
am with you: give firmness to the believers: I will instill terror
into the hearts of the unbelievers: smite ye above their necks and
smite all their finger tips off them."[33]

They but wish that ye should reject the faith, as they do, and thus be
on the same footing (as they): so take not allies from their ranks until
they flee in the way of Allah (from what is forbidden). But if they
turn renegades, seize them and slay them wherever ye find them;
and (in any case) take no allies or supporters from their ranks.[34]

With regard to the Qur'an, Muslim scholars assert that the historical
context in which these verses arose is significant as Muhammad previously
had been expelled from Mecca and denied the use of the common worship
area known as the Kaaba. In addition, the *iyat* or verse immediately following
the second quote above makes exceptions for those groups with whom there
is a peace treaty or who refrain from aggression:

Except those who join a group between whom and you there is a
treaty (of peace), or those who approach you with hearts restraining
them from fighting you as well as fighting their own people. If Allah
had pleased, He could have given them power over you, and they
would have fought you: therefore if they withdraw from you but
fight you not, and (instead) send you (guarantees of) peace, then
Allah hath opened no way for you (to war against them).[35]

Despite their context, the endorsement of violence in these holy books
should not be condoned in the twenty-first century. Whether found in the

Bible or the Qur'an, such bellicose passages in scripture are carryovers from an ancient epoch when ethnic tribes competed for land, sought to preserve bloodlines, and fought to establish religious and cultural identity. It was a mentality that may have served a socio-evolutionary purpose at the time but is still with us today in the form of extreme patriotism and classism. In our global interdependent society, such self-centered ethnic and nationalistic identities are obsolete and a threat to international cooperation and stability. Our global village, as Marshall McLuhan referred to it, demands we identify ourselves with what Bishop William E. Swing has called our global family.[36] We are all related through our common DNA, all citizens of planet earth.

Many mainstream Christians, while they accept the books of Numbers and Deuteronomy as canonized scripture, reject the bellicose messages contained in these texts. They believe that over the centuries, people of faith have matured in their spiritual understanding. As social and political conditions evolved, humanity's conception of divinity deepened and became more enlightened. The Supreme Being is viewed today among mainline Christians as a god of mercy who transforms humanity through love and sacrifice rather than through punishment and violence.

The Qur'an describes God as merciful and compassionate in its opening surah. As revealed earlier, it also assures readers that devout Jews and Christians have nothing to fear on Judgment Day.[37] The Qur'an even goes further when it speaks against religious coercion:

> Let there be no compulsion [coercion] in religion. Truth stands
> out clear from error: whoever rejects Evil and believes in God hath
> grasped the most trustworthy handhold, that never breaks.[38]

Thus, there are no social or theological reasons for Muslims to war against or seek to convert sincere believers who embrace the concept of a supreme god. The Qur'an itself provides Muslims a theological basis for understanding jihad primarily as an inner nonviolent struggle whereby mercy and compassion are given power to overcome anger and hate.

Apocalyptic Metaphors

Those who warn of a nuclear apocalypse often speak of the "fire of judgment." This image finds expression in chapter 4 of the biblical prophet Malachi:

For behold, the day comes, burning like an oven, when all the arrogant and all evil doers will be stubble; the day that comes shall burn them up, says the Lord of Hosts.[39]

In the Gospel of Luke, Jesus invokes the metaphor of fire when he says, "I came to cast fire upon the earth."[40] It is amusing to consider how a literal interpretation of this verse would render Jesus to be a raging pyromaniac! It is obvious to the rational reader that Jesus was not speaking literally but was referring to spiritual fire such as that which descended on the apostles at Pentecost.*

Perhaps the most convincing argument supporting a nonviolent interpretation of the end-times is the actual meaning of the term *apocalypse*. Its linguistic derivation does not connote human-inflicted mass destruction; rather, its meaning is derived from the Greek word meaning "uncovering" or "unveiling." The metaphors of veil and covering are used by the prophet Isaiah who writes, "And the Lord will destroy on this mountain the covering that is cast over all peoples, the veil that is spread over all nations."[41] The apostle Paul also applies this metaphor when he describes the veil that lies over the minds of those bound by the law of Moses and what Paul refers to as the old covenant.[42] The apostle then explains that "when a man turns to the Lord, the veil is removed . . . And we all, with unveiled face, are changed into his likeness from one degree of glory to another."[43]

The use of the veil metaphor is also found in Hinduism as it relates to the concept of maya or illusion. Maya is often depicted as a veil that shrouds the soul.[44] When enlightenment dawns, this veil is removed, enabling one to

---

*   Christians who are reluctant to depart from a literal interpretation of scripture should consult Galatians 4:22-26. In these verses, the apostle Paul interprets the story of Abraham and the birth of his two sons as an allegory, ascribing symbolic significance to Hager, his slave, and Sarah, his barren wife. "For it is written that Abraham had two sons, one by a slave and one by a free woman. But the son of the slave was born according to the flesh, the son of the free woman through promise. Now this is an allegory: these women are two covenants. One is from Mount Sinai, bearing children for slavery; she is Hagar. Now Hagar is Mount Sinai in Arabia; she corresponds to the present Jerusalem, for she is in slavery with her children. But the Jerusalem above is free, and she is our mother." Thus, symbolic interpretation of scripture is exemplified in the apostle Paul's exegesis.

perceive reality from a heightened state of awareness free from the influence of selfish desire and unconscious bias.

In popular Christian culture, the myth of the literal rapture served as a basis for the bestselling book *Left Behind* by Tim LaHaye and Jerry B. Jenkins. In subsequent years, this novel inspired several sequels and a popular movie by the same name. The Gospel of Matthew includes the following verses that have helped perpetuate this myth:

> Then two men will be in the field; one is taken and one is left. Two women will be grinding at the mill; one is taken and one is left. Watch therefore, for you do not know on what day your Lord is coming.[45]

Hindu commentators provide us with a meaningful symbolic interpretation of this passage. They apply their experience that each person possesses a dual nature. Using Western terminology, this dual nature can be described as a lower, psychological "self," and a higher spiritual "Self" (designated with a capital *S* in English translation), which in Indian philosophy is referred to as Atman. Each "self" coexists within everyone like two birds perched on the self-same tree, the lower bird enjoying the fruits of this life while the higher bird looks on as a witness.[46] Hindu sages assert that in the gospel passage found in Matthew, the one taken and the one that is left are actually the same person.[47]

In the mystical experience, it is the lower self that is "left behind" as the higher spiritual "Self" ascends so as to experience union with the Divine. This interpretation views the verses in Matthew's gospel as a metaphor for an inner experience and is truer to the meaning of the word *rapture*, which *Webster's Dictionary* defines as a "state of being carried away with love, joy, etc.; extreme delight, transport, ecstasy." It is also compatible with Jesus' teaching that the "Kingdom of God is within you" or "in your midst,"[48] as opposed to existing as a place above or distant from oneself.*

---

* The Revised Standard Version of the Bible translates the last phrase of this passage as "the Kingdom of God is in your midst." The original Greek text, as found in the Alfred Marshall Interlinear Greek-English New Testament, reads "within you." Despite the difference in translations, either rendering depicts heaven as an immediate and accessible reality rather than as a place enjoyed only by departed souls.

These and other interpretations discussed in this chapter support a nonviolent understanding of apocalypse, one that allows for the fulfillment of apocalyptic visions in various religious traditions without the occurrence of war. Such an apocalypse would consist of a shared, collective realization symbolized in the Gospel of Matthew by the "lightning" that "comes from the east and shines as far as the west."[49, *] The veil of ignorance that leads humanity deeper and deeper into darkness will then be lifted, freeing us from delusions brought on by anger, hatred, and the belief that violence must inevitably be used to overcome evil.

Armageddon and the Mahabharata

The book of Revelation names Armageddon as the place where the great final battle occurs between the nations of the earth near the end of time. It is during this battle that Christ is to return for the purpose of saving the elect in preparation for the descent of the "New Jerusalem" and the creation of "a new heaven and a new earth."[50] Most interpreters see this ultimate confrontation at Armageddon as unique to the writer's prophecy. However, the idea of a battle within which a heroic messianic figure plays a pivotal role existed at least five hundred years before the birth of Christianity.

At the center of the great Indian epic known as the *Mahabharata*, there is a scripture, cherished by Hindus, known as the Bhagavad Gita, the title of which means "Lord's song." At this point in the story, two huge armies have positioned themselves for war to settle a family dispute over who should rule the kingdom. On one side is King Yudhisthira, who has lost his throne. Arjuna, the great archer-warrior, leads his army. Lord Krishna, who in Hinduism is viewed as a divine incarnation or avatar, guides Arjuna in his chariot.

The battle that ensues lasts eighteen days and results in great carnage. It is, one could say, the Armageddon of the *Mahabharata*. Arjuna and his army, with Lord Krishna by his side, emerge victorious, and King Yudhisthira is restored to his rightful throne.

---

*   Hindu scripture also uses the lightning metaphor, the Chandogya Upanishad describing Brahman as "He who dwells in the sky and makes lightning his home" (Prabhavananda & Manchester, *The Upanishads*, 67).

After the battle, a sage named Narada appears to King Yudhisthira and asks, "Sir, through Krishna's grace, the valour of Arjuna and the power of your dharma, you were victorious and you are sovereign Lord of the Land. Are you happy?"

Yudhisthira responds, saying, "It is true the kingdom has come into my possession. But my kinsmen are all gone. We have lost sons that were dear. This victory appears to me but a great defeat . . . . This terrible act of slaying our own brothers was the result of our sinful attachment to our possessions."[51] The concluding message of the *Mahabharata* then is quite clear: victory in war is, in actuality, a great defeat for humanity.

Let us then take a lesson from this great Hindu epic. If a modern-day Armageddon does occur, particularly if it involves a nuclear exchange as many religious fundamentalists predict, there will be no miraculous transformation of the earth as envisioned in the book of Revelation.[52] There will be no descent of a New Jerusalem from heaven above, no idyllic Earth reappearing before us. Rather, there will be mass destruction, carnage, disease, and death on a scale that dwarfs Hiroshima, Nagasaki, Katrina, and the 2004 Asian tsunami. We would be left with a world that would take decades, perhaps even centuries, to rebuild. Indeed, such an Armageddon would be humanity's greatest defeat.*

We must then ask the question, are we sane human beings? If so, we have no choice but to pursue a nonviolent apocalypse. Interfaith organizations such as the United Religions Initiative† actively seek to end religiously motivated violence by promoting constructive dialogue and cooperation between faith traditions. Such organizations can assist people of faith in developing theologies that reject violence, respect the discoveries of science, and equip moderate mainstream clergy with the knowledge to defend the symbolic interpretation of scripture. For the Greek word from which the term *apocalypse* is derived means "uncovering" or "unveiling" and does not inherently imply calamity or violence. It therefore is possible for the world to undergo a nonviolent apocalypse, a paradigm shift triggered by a collective

---

*   During his arrest in the Garden of Gethsemane, Jesus rebukes one of his disciples for cutting off the ear of the slave of the high priest, saying, "Put your sword back into its place; for all who take the sword will perish by the sword" (Matt. 26:52). Clearly, Jesus is applying this proverb to his closest followers as well as to their enemies.

†   See appendix 1 for information on international interfaith organizations.

realization that unveils within each individual the divine image in which everyone is created. This is our common humanity, and its recognition enables us to perceive the unity that transcends ethnic, religious, and nationalistic divisions.

One ultimately comes to realize that the soul has no color, that the only "race" is the human race. Whether one believes in the biblical Adam or an evolutionary "Lucy,"* the conclusion is the same; we are all descended from the same source. We are all cousins, sharing the same blood types and the same genetic code.

The use of apocalyptic language by political leaders is a misguided attempt to use religion to legitimize violence. Martial images in scripture are best interpreted as symbols that depict an inner struggle whereby we are freed from destructive emotions that give rise to religious intolerance and ethnic prejudice. To use the mystical language of the apostle Paul, the "veil" that covers our minds must be removed[53] so that "we shall not all sleep, but we shall all be changed, in a moment in the twinkling of an eye."[54] We will then no longer "see in a mirror dimly," but ultimately behold the image of God in one another "face to face."[55] And as we shall now see in chapter 2, the spiritual path to successful nonviolence is rife with paradox.

---

*   The name given to the archeological find of a human ancestor from the genus *Australopithecus*, discovered in Africa in 1974 and dated to be approximately 3.2 million years old.

Every gun that is made, every warship launched, every rocket fired signifies, in the final sense, a theft from those who hunger and are not fed, those who are cold and are not clothed. This world in arms is not spending money alone. It is spending the sweat of its laborers, the genius of its scientists, the hopes of its children. This is not a way of life at all in any true sense. Under the cloud of threatening war, it is humanity hanging from a cross of iron.

—Dwight D. Eisenhower

Chapter 2

Nonviolence as a Spiritual Path

I think your procurator, if he were here, would agree with me when I say, this Jesus could be much more dangerous now that he's dead.
—High Priest Caphius,
from the movie *Jesus of Nazareth*

Taoist teachers and Zen masters have been known for inverting or turning upside down the values we normally associate with success in the world. They offer a paradoxical view of life referred to as *value inversion*, a philosophy eloquently expressed in the following passage from the Tao Te Ching:*

> Yield and overcome;
> Bend and be straight;
> Empty and be full;
> Wear out and be new;
> Have little and gain.[1]

Examples of value inversion are also found in Christian scripture, as in the Gospel of Matthew where Jesus is quoted as saying: "He who finds his life shall lose it. And he who loses his life for My sake shall find it."[2] Such passages express the sacrificial nature of individuals who forgo personal

---

* The Tao Te Ching is the primary scripture of Taoism. For more discussion on Taoism and its relationship to nonviolence, see chapter 5.

comforts and ambition, and devote themselves to eradicating injustice using spiritually-based nonviolence. We will now examine two well-known cases viewed through the lens of value inversion.

MLK and Gandhi

How can anyone who protests using nonviolence ever succeed in bringing about reform when they are challenging a powerful government with ready access to law enforcement and military might? Why is it that such activist leaders are not silenced or killed by authorities early in their resistance to put an end to their menace? The answer I give to these questions is that ethical nonviolent activists restrain their vengeful defense mechanisms and appeal to the moral conscience of the people. They maneuver themselves into a position where it becomes beneficial for their adversaries to let them win. In many cases, they actually become more dangerous dead than alive. Consider the following examples.

The year was 1964. Lyndon Baines Johnson was president of the United States. The civil rights movement was well underway and gathering momentum. Rev. Dr. Martin Luther King Jr., having studied the teachings of Mahatma Gandhi, was leading a nonviolent movement demanding federal legislation to guarantee equal rights for black Americans. Earlier, on August 28, 1963, King delivered his famous "I have a dream" speech in Washington DC. A crowd of over two hundred thousand civil rights activists and supporters listened intently as he spoke on the front steps of the Lincoln Memorial.

Challenging Lyndon Johnson in the presidential election campaign of 1964 was the Republican candidate, Barry Goldwater. Senator Goldwater argued that federal civil rights legislation was not necessary, pointing out that the United States constitution already granted the rights of citizenship to black Americans. "The right to vote," exclaimed the senator, "to equal treatment before the law, to hold property, and to the protection of contracts are clearly guaranteed by the Fourteenth and Fifteenth amendments to the Constitution. These rights should be rigorously enforced. Existing law demands it."[3]

For Goldwater, the enforcement of those rights was the responsibility of each individual state. His position asserted the long-standing conservative principle of states' rights.

Another important player in this sociopolitical drama was Malcolm X. As a passionate and influential black leader, he sought equal rights for black Americans but stated that "our objective is complete freedom, justice, and equality by *any means necessary.*" This included the use of violence. His view toward Martin Luther King's nonviolence was paradoxical, as Malcolm X believed he could help King by attacking him. "If the white people realize what the alternative is, perhaps they will be more willing to hear Dr. King."[4]

Which of these important figures was the Democratic incumbent, President Lyndon Johnson, in a position to support? He could hardly support Barry Goldwater; Senator Goldwater was his political opponent in the presidential race. Nor could he back the controversial Malcolm X as he then could be criticized for condoning violence and risking possible anarchy in the streets of America. He decided wisely to support Martin Luther King. King had seized the high moral ground, was appealing to the moral conscience of America, and advocated strict adherence to the principle of nonviolence.

Although Lyndon Johnson possessed a deep personal commitment to civil rights, it was King's efforts and personal sacrifice that provided President Johnson with a social mandate to push for legislation. The United States Congress passed the Civil Rights Act in 1964, followed by the Voting Rights Act in 1965. King politically had placed himself in a position where it was advantageous for the president and the United States Congress to support him and thereby let him win.

A second example is found in Mohandas K. (Mahatma) Gandhi. From 1893 to 1915, Gandhi mostly resided in South Africa which was a colony of the British Empire. There he led several civil disobedience campaigns protesting British laws that discriminated against black South Africans and the resident Indian population. He also began and supervised an Indian ambulance corps during the Second Boer War (1899-1902) when the British fought against Dutch-Afrikaner settlers in the independent Boer republics to the north. As a result of his success as an activist, British leaders were well aware of his ability to mobilize the Indian people in ways that crossed religious and cultural boundaries.

After returning to India in 1915, Gandhi became a leading figure in the Indian National Congress. He also continued his activism and began a national campaign of noncoorperation and tax resistance against British rule on the Indian subcontinent.

Gandhi soon realized, however, that many Indian citizens lacked the discipline and moral restraint to carry out successful nonviolence. In 1922, Indian citizens marching in Chauri Chaura broke into deadly rioting, an event that prompted Gandhi's penitential fast in February of that same year. To the frustration of Jawaharlal Nehru and other Indian leaders, Gandhi called a halt to his campaign of tax resistance and noncooperation.[5] In so doing, he demonstrated to the British his influence as a sage and his ability to restrain the vengeful Indian revolutionaries poised to launch violent protests against British rule. To silence Gandhi would be to remove the primary voice among Indians calling for restraint. The most the British could do was to censure or imprison him.

Winston Churchill perhaps expressed it best in October of 1921 when he said, "It amazes me that Gandhi should be allowed to go undermining our position month after month and year after year."[6] Years later in 1943, it was Viceroy Victor Linlithgow who, during another one of Gandhi's notorious fasts while in prison, recognized that if Gandhi died, the reaction across India against the British would be far-reaching and uncontrollable.[7] Gandhi had placed himself in a position where he would be more influential, and thereby more dangerous, dead than alive.

In many countries, where violent revolutions have occurred, the transfer of power is marked by the destruction of effigies and memorials built to honor former leaders. But in India, remnants of the British past are being preserved. The majestic Victoria Memorial in Kolkata (formerly Calcutta) is a prime example. The statue of Queen Victoria still stands, but she now presides over a museum commemorating the history of the nonviolent movement inspired by Gandhi that serves as an example for the world.

Despite their teachings of nonviolence, both Mahatma Gandhi and Martin Luther King Jr. made the ultimate sacrifice. After challenging the political landscape in their respective countries, they both fell prey to assassins, and it is through death that their immortality as spiritual leaders and great historical figures was sealed.*

Peeling the Onion

In July of 2009, I ventured to Walden Pond near Concord, Massachusetts. The weather was ideal as I sauntered along the wooded shoreline path. Soon I found a secluded spot near where transcendentalist writer Henry David Thoreau built his famous cabin. Sitting beneath the native hardwoods, I enjoyed the harmony of a sublime evening breeze as I intoned a Sanskrit hymn to settle into a deep meditation, my mind savoring the clarity of awareness for

---

*   The assassinations of Gandhi and King, however, should not be used to justify volunteer martyrdom. Nonviolence implies reverence for life, and that includes reverence for one's own life. To be effective over time, activists must challenge authority yet avoid death and long-term imprisonment so they can continue to protest and work to eradicate injustice.

which the clear Walden spring water has served as metaphor. Thoreau, in his own words, describes such a meditative experience in his chapter in *Walden*, entitled "Sounds."

> Sometimes in a summer morning, having taken my accustomed bath, I sat in my sunny doorway from sunrise till noon, rapt in a revery, amidst the pines and hickories and sumachs, in undisturbed solitude and stillness, while birds sang around or flitted noiseless through the house, until by the sun falling in at my west window, or the noise of some traveller's wagon on the distant highway, I was reminded of the lapse of time. I grew in those seasons like corn in the night, and they were far better than any work of the hands would have been. They were not time subtracted from my life, but so much over and above my usual allowance.[8]

Those who practice a form of meditation or reflective prayer surely can identify with Thoreau's words. To grow "like corn in the night" is to appreciate the mystery within which epiphanies dawn, enriching life with deeper levels of meaning.

Reality, one can say, is like an onion. We must peel away layer after layer in order to arrive at its core, and in the process, we may shed some tears. Meditation is an effective way to peel the onion, to probe life experience by awakening our faculties of insight and realization. Buddhist master Thich Nhat Hanh refers to this as *vipasyana*, meaning "insight" or "looking deeply."[9] Christian contemplative Thomas Merton calls it "interior prayer," a process of reflection that involves "not only the mind but also the heart, and indeed our whole being."[10] It is a practice that enables a person to perceive and appreciate the world on more profound levels. Through meditation we come to recognize the interdependent relationships that lie beneath the superficial realms of experience, perceptions which, unlike classical science, bestow upon us interpretative wisdom rather than offer mere facts.

Many people erroneously believe that meditation causes a person to become complacent or to withdraw from life. This belief is clearly refuted by the dynamic lives of many people who meditate daily, and by the Indian scriptures that deal with the experience of spiritual enlightenment. The Isha Upanishad says, "To darkness are they doomed who devote themselves only to life in the world, and to a greater darkness are they who devote themselves only to meditation."[11] The intended meaning of this passage is that a person must find a balance between meditation and activity or "life in the world."

Thich Nhat Hanh states it even more emphatically: "Meditation is not a drug to make us oblivious to our real problems. It should produce awareness in us and also in our society."[12] The awareness that Hanh describes is both a personal and social mindfulness. We become aware of our inner strength and also of the needs of those in the world around us.

During meditation, we witness our thoughts, moods, feelings, and impulses as they arise and subside in the mind on the background of silence. When mental activity subsides during meditation for a significant period, we experience awareness by itself, or "pure consciousness." Through this practice we are awakened to our essential nature, which is beyond the intellect and ego, beyond moods and feelings, indeed, beyond the mind itself.*

In the domain of religion, the awakening experience is usually associated with Buddhism. The Dhammapada says, "The disciples of Buddha are always well awake."[13] This concept of awakening, however, is also found in Hindu and Christian scripture. The Katha Upanishad commands the disciple to "arise, awake, sit at the feet of the master and know Brahman."[14, †] In his

---

*   Mindfulness is of two types, voluntary and involuntary. Voluntary mindfulness occurs by purposeful intention; we purposefully direct our awareness to observe a simple task we are performing. Forms of walking meditation often take this approach. Involuntary mindfulness occurs extemporaneously. We become engaged in an activity and unintentionally find ourselves spontaneously witnessing our actions. Generally, involuntary mindfulness is first experienced during meditation (see appendix 2) as certain forms of meditation cultivate the witnessing experience, first on the level of thoughts and feelings, and later outside of meditation during waking activity. Eventually, one has the experience of witnessing dreams and deep sleep. In *Walden,* Henry David Thoreau poetically describes this witnessing consciousness: "However intense my experience, I am conscious of the presence and criticism of a part of me, which as it were, is not a part of me, but spectator, sharing no experience, but taking note of it; and that is no more I than it is you. When the play, it may be the tragedy, of life is over, the spectator goes his way. It was a kind of fiction, a work of the imagination only so far as he was concerned." (Thoreau. *Walden,* with an introduction and annotations by Bill McKribben, 127-128).

†   In Hinduism, Brahman is the Ultimate Reality to be realized by the earnest seeker of Truth. It is paradoxically referred to in the Kena Upanishad as "that which cannot be seen, but by which the eye sees . . . That which cannot be heard, but by which the ear hears . . . That which cannot be comprehended by the mind, but by which the mind comprehends" (Prabhavananda and Manchester, *The Upanishads,* 30-31).

letter to the Ephesians, the apostle Paul declares, "Awake, O sleeper and rise from the dead, and Christ will give thee light."[15] In the Gospel of Mark, Jesus expresses this in the negative, cautioning his disciples not to be caught sleeping: "Watch therefore, for you do not know when the Master of the house will come . . . lest he come suddenly and find you asleep."[16, *]

Inherent to this awakening experience is the understanding of what we call spirit. It is the spirit that exalts and inspires. It instills within us a sense of wholeness and a higher, more inclusive level of awareness whereby we experience the ineffable and recognize the whole as greater than the sum of its parts. One becomes a visionary with a positive sense of purpose and the power to manifest one's vision. The spirit is that potent life-energy that enables us to exceed our expectations, to experience what psychologist Abraham Maslow called the peak experience. Moreover, it is the spirit that distinguishes the creative transformational intelligence in humans from the preprogrammed artificial intelligence of machines.

Although I have been quoting mostly from religious texts and the writings of spiritual teachers, the awakening experience is also accessible to the secular humanist. The mind is opened to fresh possibilities. Reason is freed from conformity. We become receptive to the underlying silence deep within, that womb from which insights and realizations are born. Peace educator Michael N. Nagler, author of *The Search for a Nonviolent Future*, explains it as follows:

> The student doesn't just learn some facts, doesn't just learn how
> to put facts together, but awakens to a new realization. It is more
> a growth experience than just acquiring knowledge, and after *this*
> kind of learning, one does not go back to sleep.[17]

From the perspective of nonviolence, not going "back to sleep" means being awake to an injustice and inspired to take action to expose and address it. The insights acquired through reflective prayer and meditation answer our query for the most effective strategies as we pursue a higher cause outside our comfort zone. Such insights are not merely intellectual or rational. They move us as empathetic human beings, spurring us to act so as to right the wrong and establish policies and conditions that are fair and equitable to all.

---

*   I propose there are nine pivotal awakenings in the growth of human consciousness. For further discussion, see appendix 3.

The key to success once an injustice is identified is to address the inequitable condition in its infancy, well before a conflict reaches the apex of violent confrontation. We become skilled at anticipating the danger that has yet to come. In addition, we must work to establish and maintain social, political, and economic institutions that will listen and respond to the appeal for change.

Unfortunately, people often fear change and resist opportunities for reform. In addition to the uncertainty it brings, change reminds us that everything in this world is transitory, including ourselves. We are thereby confronted with our own transience, and our own mortality. Laying the foundation for a future without war requires us to overcome this fear.

Spiritual Fire

When people associate nonviolence with spirituality, they often bring to mind the moral principles common to the great world religions—teachings such as the golden rule, "love your neighbor as yourself," pray for your enemies, or the importance of cultivating compassion. Although these teachings serve as a foundation for the practice of nonviolence, they alone are not what I mean when I refer to nonviolence as a spiritual path.

To the surprise of most people, I view nonviolence as a personal battle in which the individual activist is willing to risk the potential consequences of speaking out against injustice. You have not experienced the spiritual value of nonviolence until you receive hate mail or obscene phone calls. You have not experienced the spiritual value of nonviolence until you fear you may lose your job, are publicly slandered, or have your property vandalized. These are just a few of the risks one takes for speaking publicly on behalf of those who are oppressed. Once you have been awakened to this kind of hatred and endured its emotional impact, knowing that you have spoken the truth, you soon come to realize the meaning of the verse: "Blessed are those who are persecuted for righteousness' sake, for yours is the kingdom of heaven."[18] While the persecution you endure may be psychological rather than physical, the blessing you receive for your fortitude is self-respect, strength of character, and the future admiration of those who lacked the courage to make themselves heard.

During my stays in India, I saw the extreme conditions in which many people lived, conditions that I had been insulated from as a child. I was continually jolted back and forth, my experience alternating between abject poverty and excessive affluence, crass commercialism and the most refined art and music, mundane conversation and deep philosophical discourse. In India, one encounters, on a daily basis, religious icons that evoke within one's consciousness the fundamental forces of nature and concerns in life. Among these concerns are wealth, fertility, death, creation, preservation, destruction, education, moral order, righteousness, and the removal of obstacles to fulfillment. Perhaps the most prominent icon is that of the deity Shiva (Nataraja in South India), the bringer of enlightenment and destroyer of ignorance, who is depicted as dancing within a ring of fire.

Fire has been used in various religions to represent the spiritual force that tests, purifies, and transforms the seeker. A fire burns in the heart of every Zoroastrian temple. In Judaism, the prophet Malachi speaks of the Lord's messenger as someone who will purify the sons of Levi like a refiner's fire,[19] and in Christianity, it was the fire of the Holy Spirit that descended on the apostles at Pentecost. This spiritual fire, however, is not a cozy campfire around which people sit to share stories or sing hymns. Rather, it troubles us within, tempers our character and strengthens our resolve, calling us to take action to fulfill a task for which we have been chosen.

In Greek mythology, Prometheus evoked the ire of the gods when he stole fire from heaven and brought it to earth. As a consequence, he was stretched out and chained to a rock while an eagle, sent by Zeus, would gnaw at his liver. In the context of nonviolence, it was not literal fire that Prometheus won for humanity. It was the fire that unveils truth and, in doing so, challenges injustice and makes it visible. It is the weapon of the whistle-blower—the courageous person who exposes wrongdoing and, as a result, suffers retribution from those intent on concealing the truth. Once you experience this Promethean fire, you will understand why the practice of nonviolence is a spiritual path.

Like Prometheus, Jesus brought spiritual fire, challenging the authorities of his time, and his fate was not unlike that of Prometheus. But instead of a rock, Jesus was stretched out on a cross; instead of an eagle, it was a spear that impaled his liver.* Recognizing the power of the Prometheus myth, Ralph Waldo Emerson, in his essay "History," refers to this Greek

---

*   In artistic renditions, the wound in Christ's side is traditionally placed over the liver as indicated by the descriptive phrase in John's gospel, "There came out blood and water" (John 19:34). The *water* in this passage is believed to refer to bile. It may be significant that the account of Jesus being pierced by the spear only occurs in the Gospel of John. John's gospel begins by equating Christ with the Greek concept of Logos (translated as "Word" in John 1:1). Could it be the apostle was intentionally evoking the Promethean image to appeal to those familiar with Greek philosophy and mythology?

hero as the "Jesus of old mythology."[20] It is the Promethean fire that brings enlightenment and exposes injustice, making a person more influential, and eventually more dangerous, dead than alive. For the influence of such individuals, from Jesus to Gandhi to Martin Luther King, lives on just as the sun continues to shine even through the darkest and most violent periods of human history. *

The Threat of Innocence

How could nonviolent resistance be so effective as to be feared by political leaders? With respect to British colonialism, historian Arthur Herman addresses this question eloquently in his dual biography of Gandhi and Churchill:

> Violence and armed force, even insurrection, were something the British knew how to deal with. Noncooperation on a massive scale was something else again. Even in 1909 Winston Churchill realized that saving the British Empire in India meant halting a visionary like Gandhi in his tracks.[21]

The threat of massive noncooperation against political power, however, when activists remain innocent of violent behavior, is a fear alluded to in religious myth dating back 2,500 years.

---

* In their quest to discover what actually happened to the historical Jesus, commentators often fail to recognize that in the gospels, those calling for Christ's crucifixion are a metaphor for all of humanity. We are in search of our origin, our creator. Yet when the creator appears, we do not recognize the divine embodiment. In our ignorance, we see only the superficial human form and fail to perceive the deeper divinity within. This is expressed in the Gospel of John where it says, "He [Christ] was in the world and the world was made through him, yet the world knew him not" (John 1:10). A similar message is found in the *Bhagavad Gita* where the divine Krishna says, "This world is deluded and does not recognize me" (Ch. VII:25).

That the incarnate Lord in the Christian allegory is then tortured and executed as a common criminal by his own people is a statement of the depth of human ignorance. Not only do we not recognize the Divine, we persecute and take vengeance against it. Not only do we take vengeance, we seek to kill it; but as we shall learn in Chapter 7, the Divine cannot be killed, neither can the influence of the life it inspires.

The Indian Purana known as the Srimad Bhagavatam, tells the story of Lord Krishna's birth to his mother Devaki. As a divine incarnation, his birth auspiciously occurs when the star Rohini was in the ascent. Soon after he is born, Krishna is taken to a remote village where he is raised by cowherds. The reason for this flight was to hide the child from Kamsa, the jealous king who fears Krishna's destiny is to destroy him. Kamsa is firmly committed to finding and killing the child. At a meeting of his advisors, the king is told that the only way to insure the child is dead is to "destroy all children around us who are less than a year old." Kamsa then orders the village children to be massacred.[22]

A comparable story in Christian scripture is known as the slaughter of the innocents. In the Gospel of Matthew, the king is Herod the Great who governs Judea. He is visited by Magi, or wise men from Persia who ask where they would find the newborn "King of the Jews," whose star they had seen "in the East."[23] Like King Kamsa in the Hindu text, King Herod fears an innocent child. Joseph, the husband of Mary, the mother of Jesus, is warned in a dream to take the infant Jesus to Egypt to escape Herod's wrath. Herod soon orders all male children in Bethlehem who are under two years of age to be killed.[24, *]

Many historians and theologians doubt that the slaughter of children included in the Gospel of Matthew actually occurred. Josephus, a Jewish historian of the time, never mentions the event, nor is the massacre

---

*   After consulting his court scholars, King Herod directs the Magi to the town of Bethlehem, requesting they return to tell him where the Christ child is so he too could "come and worship him" (Matt. 2:8). The Magi then go to Bethlehem where they find the infant Jesus. After presenting gifts of gold, frankincense, and myrrh, the Magi have a dream warning them to depart to their homeland without revisiting Herod, as the king was planning to slay the child.

Why could not the Magi have had a dream telling them where the Christ child was to be born before they visited Herod in the first place? The likely allegorical meaning is that in following the "star," the Magi were being guided by a light external to themselves. The Christ child represents the divine light within. Once the Magi found the Christ child, they then could be guided by their inner light, the source of wisdom and epiphanies. They could now have a dream, which was their epiphany, telling them to change directions and proceed via a different path.

recorded in any of the other gospels.* Furthermore, it does seem unlikely that a powerful ruler like Herod would feel threatened by a mere child. If we consider this an example of mythmaking, what could be the intended allegorical meaning of the story and the similar Hindu rendition attached to the birth of Krishna?

Myths such as these are meant to expose the darkest side of human nature and the desperate psychological need of authoritarian leaders to control the masses. Like the innocence of a helpless babe, the charismatic prophet and the movement he or she inspires are a great threat to powerful political and military leaders, even to the point where those in power are willing to commit genocide. One atrocity that illustrates this is the massacre at Amritsar, India, on April 13, 1919.

British brigadier general Reginald Dyer, fearing a possible uprising and trying to enforce a ban on public meetings, ordered his troops to fire on a crowd of innocent, unarmed civilians that had gathered in a garden near Amritsar's Sikh Golden Temple. According to the British, the number killed totaled close to 400 while over 1,200 were wounded. A separate inquiry by the Indian National Congress, however, estimated the number killed at 1,000. The casualties included many women and children.[25] The event marked a crucial turning point in British-Indian relations. Public sentiment toward the British from then on was unforgiving and never recovered.[26]

Mahatma Gandhi made certain the massacre would not be forgotten. His efforts to make it public knowledge eventually led to an inquiry in late 1919 known as Hunter Commission. In responding to the commission, General Dyer stated, "I think it quite possible that I could have dispersed the crowd without firing, but they would have come back again and laughed, and I would have made, what I consider, a fool of myself." Months later, on July 8, 1920, there was a showdown in the British House of Commons between Winston Churchill and Dyer's supporters. Churchill recounted the cold-blooded brutality of the general's orders in a speech that essentially ended Dyer's military career.[27] When Gandhi orchestrated his famous march to the sea to make salt eleven years later, the Mahatma made it a point to arrive at the beach town of Dandi in April, close to the anniversary of the massacre.

---

*   Some writers believe the slaughter in Bethlehem to be an actual historical event. They propose that historians do not mention this massacre, claiming it was small compared to other atrocities King Herod committed during his reign.

Innocence is like a mirror that reflects evil back onto itself. The Amritsar massacre is what General Reginald Dyer is remembered for, despite any good deeds he may have done in his life. As the Buddha is credited with saying:

> A wicked man who reproaches a virtuous one is like one who looks up and spits at heaven; the spittle soils not the heaven, but comes back and defiles his own person. The slanderer is like one who flings dust at another when the wind is contrary; the dust does but return on him who threw it.[28]

Paradoxically, it is because of the threat of innocence that visionaries devoted to forgiveness and reconciliation can be such a potent force of transformation. Theirs is an ongoing struggle to restore justice in our fractured world.

If you are neutral in situations of injustice, you have chosen the side of the oppressor. If an elephant has its foot on the tail of a mouse and you say that you are neutral, the mouse will not appreciate your neutrality.

—Bishop Desmond Tutu

Chapter 3

The Quest for Justice

War is the greatest of all crimes: and yet there is no aggressor who does not color his crime with the pretext of justice.
> —Francois Marie Arouet Voltaire

Pope Paul VI, known for his ecumenical outreach and his eloquent peace activism, made a simple but influential statement in a speech delivered on January 1, 1972: "If you want peace, work for justice." His address was for the celebration of the Day of Peace and took place at the height of the Vietnam War at a time when the issue of civil rights in the United States was politically divisive. The saying eventually became a popular slogan embraced by peace activists both within and outside the Catholic church.*

Years ago, my initial reaction was to view this aphorism as an eloquent truism. It seems obvious that peace must be dependent on equal opportunity and the rule of law being impartially applied by a trusted government and legal system. How could there not be peace if justice is served to the satisfaction of all conflicting parties?

On the other hand, the absence of peace often creates conditions where injustice and political corruption thrive. Walter Kendall III, professor at the John Marshall Law School in Chicago, suggests that it is perhaps equally

---

* Over two centuries earlier, Quaker leader William Penn made virtually the same assertion when he wrote, "Thus peace is maintained by justice" (Zinn, *The Power of Nonviolence: Writings by Advocates of Peace*, 6).

valid to state Pope Paul's aphorism in reverse: "If you want justice, work for peace."[1] Certainly, some degree of security and social order is prerequisite to creating and enforcing laws that are just and fair to all.

To complicate matters, what constitutes justice often is open for debate. For many Americans, O. J. Simpson's acquittal for the murders of Nicole Brown Simpson and Ron Goldman was a failure of law enforcement and the court system. For others, it was the legal system functioning as it should, protecting the innocent. Timothy McVey was sentenced to death for his part in the bombing of the federal building in Oklahoma City on April 19, 1995, but that can hardly be considered justice for the 168 people who died and the 680 that were injured by his act of domestic terrorism. Furthermore, some crimes are so horrendous no ethical punishment exists that could bring closure to the victims, their families, and loved ones. What punishment dispensed by any justice system could provide closure for the atrocities committed by tyrants like Joseph Stalin, Adolf Hitler, or Saddam Hussein? In such extreme cases, only if one believes in some form of judgment in an afterlife can it be said that justice might ultimately prevail.

It soon becomes clear that peace and justice cannot be established solely through legal, political, or military means. A multifaceted approach is required that considers social and religious attitudes toward violence as well as the consequences of collective and individual actions. Pope Paul VI was not suggesting there is a direct cause-and-effect interaction between justice and peace. One does not necessarily beget the other. Rather, the pursuit of justice addresses social inequities and seeks to create a climate in which people are confident their grievances will be heard. Religious organizations can then play an important moral and financial role in ameliorating those grievances by supporting counseling and mediation programs within their communities.

Peace: Four Definitions

Peace education is most concisely defined as "the study of conflict resolution through nonviolent means." Here, resolution includes reconciliation, which seeks not merely to resolve conflict but also to restore working relationships between conflicting parties. One can argue, however, that a prerequisite to reconciling is to first remove conflict from within ourselves since disputes may actually be rooted in our own inner discord. This tendency is expressed in the theory of *projection* formulated by Sigmund Freud, the founder of modern psychiatry. We perceive or imagine behaviors in other people that we subconsciously dislike in ourselves while projecting our personal flaws and repressed self-deprecation onto them. To use an analogy attributed to Jesus nineteen hundred years before Freud, we see the speck in our brother's eye, yet fail to see the log in our own eye.[2] The great Sufi poet Rumi, in the first volume of his *Mathnawi*, verse 1328, expresses it this way: "Many of the faults you see in others, dear reader, are your own nature reflected in them."

In the Gospel of John, when Jesus says to his disciples, "Peace I leave with you, my peace I give to you,"[3] the society in which he was teaching was hardly peaceful. The Romans occupied the land and ruled with a rod of iron,* using oppression and fear to subjugate the people. The words of Jesus, therefore, are understood to refer to an inner peace, a state of mind his disciples could experience as free from inner conflict despite the dangers present in their outer world.

This inner peace, however, is not gained by withdrawing from the world. We cannot be at peace by ignoring the injustice around us. The peace of which Jesus is speaking is perhaps better understood as resulting from being "true to oneself." It requires a person to act to improve the lives of others, to do what we can to address injustice and become an instrument for change.

From Hindu scripture comes another view of inner peace. In chapter 2, verse 70 of the Bhagavad Gita, Lord Krishna says, "He attains peace, into whom all desires flow as waters into the sea, which though ever being filled, is ever motionless and not he who lusts after desires."[4] This verse defines inner peace as a condition where one is free from desire. Here desire is usually interpreted as craving. In a state of craving, we feel separate from something we covet, whether it be a material object, physical gratification, or personal power. There is an anxiety present, a lack of fulfillment, a longing for something you perceive as missing from your life. In that lack of fulfillment, there cannot be complete peace within.

Meditation is a means of allowing the mind to settle into the state of awareness where cravings are no longer present. The experience is one of inner contentment and should not be interpreted as a condition where desires are repressed. Sitting in the sunlight, you do not find yourself

---

* It is ironic that the phrase "Rule them with a rod of iron" is also used in the book of Revelation to describe how the warrior Christ will rule over his kingdom on earth when he returns (Rev. 19: 14-16). This is quite contrary to Christ's teaching of nonviolent resistance as will be discussed in chapter 4.

desiring a candle. The fullness of the sunlight makes even the thought of a candle irrelevant. Likewise, meditation dispels worldly cravings and selfish intentions that distract us from attending to the needs of others. It enables one to experience a deeply settled mind. Daily practice results in what may be referred to as a *personal peace*.

Unrestrained anger gives rise to harmful and counterproductive thoughts and actions. It causes one to be blind to constructive alternatives. The settled meditative mind allows the negative energy behind anger to be transformed into the positive manifestation of compassion, understanding, and effective action. Meditation, therefore, should be thought of as a basis for action. It is analogous to an archer pulling the bowstring back so the arrow can be released with maximum focus and energy. Through meditation, one is awakened to perceive more deeply, gaining insight and wisdom; through activity, one attains fulfillment in the world by mindfully observing, learning from, and following one's insights.

In addition to experiencing peace as freedom from inner conflict, two further definitions of peace have been proposed by Norwegian peace researcher Johan Galtung. The first is called *negative peace*.[5]

Generally defined as the absence of war, negative peace is a condition where hostilities are either not present or are unexpressed. In its crudest form, coexisting parties or nations simply tolerate one another, making little or no effort to develop friendship, build trust, or improve the relationship. One can argue that such a condition is potentially unstable because a breakdown in tolerance can leave in its wake social or political tensions, arousing suspicions that can generate unrest. For the most part during the cold war era, the United States and the Soviet Union coexisted in a state of negative peace. Their distrust manifested itself in the costly nuclear arms race that ensued for more than three decades.

We can also, however, define peace in the positive. What Galtung calls *positive peace* is not simply the absence of hostility. Rather, a cooperative relationship is present between any two parties, whether the parties consist of individuals, social groups, or nations. According to David Barash and Charles Webel, positive peace is "a social condition in which exploitation is minimized or eliminated, and in which there is neither overt violence nor the more subtle phenomenon of underlying structural violence."[6]

Politicians who favor military intervention and often speak of going to war to establish peace are generally thinking in terms of negative peace. In contrast, peace activists are people who seek to build cooperative relationships. They invariably think in terms of positive peace. When debating the question of whether to use military force, misunderstandings frequently arise between peace activists and people who favor war because their respective positions are based on different definitions of peace.

Positive peace is a condition where there exists a sustained and developing collaborative relationship. It serves as a deterrent to hostile speech and action as the parties benefiting from the condition of positive peace do not want to jeopardize the benefits they are gaining from the relationship. Two countries that establish a productive trade relationship or support student and faculty educational exchange programs, for example, are engaged in a form of positive peace-building. The United States, England, France, Belgium, Germany, Japan, South Korea, India, Australia, and Saudi Arabia are some examples of countries that have actively engaged in economic, educational, and cultural peace-building over the past sixty years. In addition, positive peace efforts are supported through the distribution of humanitarian aid such as occurred in response to the 2004 Asian tsunami and the devastating earthquakes that occurred in Haiti and Chile in 2010.

To these definitions of peace, I add the concept of *proactive peace*. We must recognize that positive peace can occur fortuitously. If it can happen simply as the result of a convergence of beneficial circumstances, it can also deteriorate as those circumstances unexpectedly change. The practice of proactive peace requires that we (1) anticipate future economic, environmental, and political forces that could threaten to dismantle productive relations between social groups, communities and nations; (2) actively engage in peace-building to preserve cooperative working relationships; and (3) strive to correct social injustice at its inception before it reaches a crisis point. Efforts to engage citizens in interfaith fellowship and dialogue, and study circles aimed at improving race relations are examples of proactive efforts to develop and sustain positive peace at the community level.

Besides the four definitions discussed thus far, there is yet another approach to understanding the complexities of peace. Rather than thinking of peace in negative and positive terms, some researchers prefer to make clear distinctions between the concepts of peace-building, peacemaking, and peacekeeping. This approach is evident in the *Statement of Conscience on Creating Peace* adopted in 2010 by the Unitarian Universalist General Assembly. *Peace-building,* according to this document, "is the creation and support of institutions and structures that address the roots of conflict, including economic exploitation, political marginalization, the violation of human rights, and a lack of accountability to law." *Peacemaking* is defined as "the negotiation of equitable and sustainable peace agreements, mediation between hostile parties, and post-conflict rebuilding and reconciliation." *Peacekeeping* refers to "early intervention to prevent war, stop genocide, and monitor ceasefires. Peacekeeping creates the space for diplomatic efforts, humanitarian aid, and nonviolent conflict prevention through the protection of civilians and the disarmament and separation of those involved in violent conflict."[7]

Clearly, there are many avenues that can be taken to gain insight into the powerful concept of peace, all of which have their role to play in helping humanity build a future without war.

Violence: Three Definitions

As we can define peace in different ways, so there are also multiple ways to define violence. Initially, most people think of violence as action intended to cause physical harm. This definition of *physical violence* is certainly self-explanatory. Many times we forget, however, that violence can be solely of a psychological nature.

*Psychological violence** is present when a person is experiencing emotional hostility, threats, intimidation, name-calling, verbal abuse, or forms of passive aggression. This type of violence is the easiest to participate in and the most difficult to restrict because intimidation, name-calling and verbal abuse are usually protected as free speech. Bullying, which is sometimes a serious problem in schools, can take the form of psychological violence. In addition, domestic violence within a family may not always be physically abusive, yet it can be as traumatic and psychologically debilitating to its victims.

Psychological violence can have a more lasting impact than physical violence. As it says in the *Mahabharata*, "The wounds inflicted by weapons may close with time; scalds may heal gradually; but wounds inflicted by words remain painful as long as one lives."[8]

There is also the psychological impact of exposure to violence. For soldiers in combat, this impact often goes underreported until it surfaces as a spike in the number of soldiers suffering from post-traumatic stress disorder or who commit suicide.† Casualties reported in war generally only cover the number of people killed or wounded. The psychological casualties,

---

* Psychological violence is also referred to as emotional violence.

† As the wars in Iraq and Afghanistan dragged on, United States Army officials saw a steady rise in soldier suicides from 2004 to 2008 (Jerelinek, Pauline. "Army Says

both military and civilian, who may not have serious physical injuries, may still have to live with mental and emotional trauma.

Experts cannot easily quantify, diagnose, and treat the psychological impact of violence, which can manifest as alcohol and drug addiction, domestic abuse, and broken marriages among soldiers returning from war. Nor do those of us who have never been in a war zone fully realize the psychological and social damage to children orphaned by military violence. The military term *collateral damage* is meant to obscure the direct and horrific impact war has on civilians caught in the line of fire. Overall, the psychological effects of violence are not adequately recognized or reported, especially in war.

A third type of violence is known as *structural violence*. This occurs when a political, social, or economic structure disenfranchises a certain group of people by depriving them of their basic needs or denying them equal opportunity.[9] A political system that does not have laws against child labor, for example, tolerates structural violence when businesses and corporations employ underage children. Child laborers suffer impaired physical, emotional, and social growth. Children caught in systems that use underage labor are often denied access to education and, subsequently, access to a better life in adulthood. Structural violence also occurs in societies that restrict the rights of women. Historically, this has been the case in countries and religious institutions where women cannot attain the same economic, educational, and leadership opportunities available to men. Barash and Webel broaden the definition of structural violence to include hunger, the lack of health care, inadequate housing and the denial of fundamental human rights.

> When people starve to death, or even go hungry, a kind of violence is taking place. Similarly, when humans suffer from diseases that are preventable, when they are denied decent education, affordable housing, opportunities to work, play, raise a family, and freedom of expression and peaceful assembly, a kind of violence is occurring, even if no bullets are shot or clubs wielded . . . Structural violence is a serious form of social oppression.[10]

Structural violence is often intentional, as in cases of racial, gender, or religious discrimination, but it also can be unintentional. When Hurricane

---

Suicides Among Soldiers at Highest Level in Decades." *The Boston Globe*, January 30, 2009).

Katrina hit New Orleans in 2005, it became painfully apparent that many of the people who became Katrina's victims were the city's working poor. These were individuals who held jobs but could not afford access to private cars or public transportation to evacuate the city, leaving them trapped in a breakdown of social and government services. Some theorists argue that structural violence is ultimately the root cause of all conflict. For this reason, many peace and justice organizations sponsor programs that fight poverty, hunger, and various forms of human and environmental exploitation. Regardless of the country or the politico-economic system, structural violence is widespread, and it is the obligation of us all to publicly address its inequalities with the goal of initiating reforms.

The Fallacy of Just War

A doctrine frequently invoked in times of military conflict is that of *just war*. Initially, just war doctrine consisted of two sets of criteria: *jus ad bellum* or rules for determining whether a country should go to war, and *jus in bello*, which consists of rules of engagement to be observed during war. Recent theorists propose a third category be added to just war doctrine, this being *jus post bellum*, which seeks to insure justice is adhered to in peace treaties and during the period of reconstruction that takes place after a war.

Examples of rules stipulated under the first criterion are as follows: the war must be declared by a legitimate authority, it must be undertaken with the right intention, the war must be a last resort, the response or retaliation must be proportionate to the aggression, and the war must have a reasonable chance of success. Rules to be followed during a war provide immunity to noncombatants, prohibit the killing of civilians, and require that the benefits of the war outweigh the damage it will cause.

Just war doctrine has a long history in the Roman Catholic Church with its most notable early proponents being St. Augustine (354-430 CE) and St. Thomas Aquinas (1225-1274 CE). Both lived during times when wars were fought primarily with swords, crossbows, and catapults. Plenty of open spaces away from population centers were available to serve as battlefields. There were no multi-megaton bombs, no complex international alliances, no United Nations, and no debates over unilateral versus multilateral decision-making.

In the 1930s, Roman Catholic activist Dorothy Day, editor of *The Catholic Worker*, was among the first to take a stand against the "immorality of conscription" and just war doctrine.[11] Pope Pius XII later offered a more reserved assessment of just war, saying that in modern warfare, the criteria of proportionality could not be met and that the theory was out of date.[12]

Today, just war theorists continue to grapple with dilemmas posed by our complex political, economic, multicultural, and military realities. Population density and the immense power of modern weaponry make it virtually impossible to avoid civilian casualties. Even with the deployment of unmanned drones that can hit small targets with pinpoint accuracy using less powerful weapons, human error still results in far too many civilian deaths. Furthermore, over the centuries, the code of warfare has degenerated to the point where the killing of civilians—the collateral in the military phrase "collateral damage"—has become accepted as inevitable. We have become numb to the extent that civilian physical and psychological casualties, population displacement, and massive numbers of refugees lie in a war's ugly wake.

In WWII, the deadliest war to date, the number of civilian casualties exceeded 55 million.[13] This figure includes those who died from conditions of famine and diseases that were war related. The twentieth century was in fact the deadliest century in human history.

From 2003 through 2008 during the U.S.-led war with Iraq, the civilian death toll is believed to have exceeded 100 thousand. It is further estimated that 2.7 million Iraqi civilians were internally displaced while close to 2 million fled Iraq, creating refugee crises in neighboring Iran, Syria, Jordon, Lebanon, and Egypt.[14] With respect to mounting civilian casualties and population displacement, the longer a war drags on, the more unjust the war becomes, and the criterion of "a reasonable chance of success" becomes increasingly difficult to define.

People who support war often express their reasons in strategic and quantitative terms. They argue that not going to war will make conditions worse, that fewer civilians will be killed due to "smart weapons," or that the use of military force will bring a conflict to a speedier end. Such justifications, however, do not make a war "just." History demonstrates that arguments such as these in advance of war are unreliable speculations. Broad quantitative justifications mean little to a civilian couple whose child is killed by an errant bomb. For them, the war has not been just.

Finally, just war doctrine, while intended to carefully guide the church's position on war, is too often appropriated and misused by leaders intent on demonizing the enemy and promoting their own political agenda. In using it to justify violence, governments and politicians become like their enemies, engaging in the very evil they say they are trying to eradicate.

For these reasons, just war doctrine must rightfully be declared obsolete. One may argue that war is a necessary evil, or the lesser of two evils, but it is simply that, an evil, and it is wrong to claim that war is theologically or ethically just.

The Elusive Moral Arc

People who consider themselves realists often say, "No one said life was fair." It is perhaps a common experience that life can deal us a bad hand and, at times, a good one, for seemingly no reason. An apparent randomness in nature prompts us to conclude that some people are blindsided by misfortune while others just get lucky.

In the ancient world, the perception that injustice is inherent to life created the need for an afterlife and a final day of cosmic restitution. The Day of Judgment would be a time when all the wrongs are punished and righteousness is restored. Here lies the source of the vision of the world's end and the ultimate condemnation of the forces of evil that, according to prophets like Zoroaster and John of Patmos,* battle with the forces of good to corrupt the material world.

It is understandable how two thousand years ago, an ultimate conclusion to history could have been envisioned. The ruthless rule of tyrannical kings and the depth of corruption in the world seemed beyond what any human legal or governing system could correct. It would take the omniscient creator of the universe, who not only had the wisdom but also the power to rectify the damage that had been done.

Indian philosophers, however, have suggested an alternative view of time and the restoration of justice. They see creation as cyclical. In the most expansive sense, the universe undergoes a manifest phase then dissolves into its source over and over. Each manifestation is referred to as a *kalpa.* The Indian view of time also includes the cycle of the four yugas or ages. These are called *sat yuga, treta yuga, dvapara yuga, and kali yuga* and are referred to respectively as the golden, silver, bronze, and iron ages.† On a

---

* The author of the New Testament book of Revelation as identified in Revelation 1:9.

† The Vedic concept of time cycles may have influenced the writers of the biblical book of Genesis. In Indian mythology, the life span for human beings is said to differ in each age. In the current age, *kali yuga*, often referred to as the age of ignorance, the human

more immediate level, empires rise and fall, and generations are born and pass away. In nature we observe the cycle of the seasons and the cycle of day and night.

Within this cyclical view, every action sets in motion a reaction; every choice made has a consequence. Indian philosophy regards this principle of action-reaction as an exact equation, a karmic law that leaves no room for random chance. Every action bears its fruit and is returned to the actor in exact and equal measure. Justice is thereby inherent in the very structure of creation. Ralph Waldo Emerson expressed this precision in his essay "Compensation":

> Polarity, or action and reaction, we meet in every part of nature; in darkness and light; in heat and cold; in the ebb and flow or waters; in male and female.

> Superinduce magnetism at one end of a needle; the opposite magnetism takes place at the other end. If the south attracts, the north repels. To empty here, you must condense there . . .

> The theory of mechanical forces is another example. What you gain in power is lost in time . . .

> The world looks like a multiplication-table or a mathematical equation, which, turn it how you will, balances itself. Take what figure you will, its exact value, no more nor less, still returns to you. Every secret is told, every crime punished, every virtue rewarded, every wrong redressed, in silence and certainty . . .

> Cause and effect, means and ends, seed and fruit, cannot be severed; for the effect already blooms in the cause, the ends pre-exists in the means, the fruit in the seed.[15]

---

life span peaks at around 100 years. In the previous age, *dvapara yuga*, human life spanned 1,000 years. The end of dvapara yuga was marked by the mythological great flood and thereafter the human life span began to shorten. This mythology accounts for the ages given for biblical characters in Genesis such as Adam, who supposedly lived 930 years, Noah, who survived the flood and lived 950 years, and later, Abraham who, being born after the flood, lived to the age of 175.

Although not expressed so precisely in the Bible, the cyclical view of creation is nevertheless presented in certain familiar verses. The apostle Paul wrote, "For whatever a man sows, that he shall also reap."[16] The opening chapter of the book of Ecclesiastes provides us with one of the most poetic descriptions of a cyclical world.

> A generation goes, and a generation comes, but the earth remains forever. The sun rises and the sun goes down, and hastens to the place where it rises. The wind blows to the south and goes round to the north; round and round goes the wind, and on its circuits the wind returns. All streams run to the sea, but the sea is not full; to the place where the streams flow, there they flow again.[17]

The precision and reliability of the laws governing human action and reaction are difficult for many to accept because the cycles that deliver the fruit or consequences of one's actions often extend beyond a person's lifetime. Most people only perceive a portion of the cycle, an arc, so to speak, of the orbit of an action set in motion.

Martin Luther King said, "Let us realize the arc of the moral universe is long, but it bends toward justice."[18, *] His metaphor of the curving arc acknowledges that life's immediate circumstances may not seem fair or equitable to all. However, over time, with patience, nonviolent action, and the practice of virtue, justice and a sense of moral conscience emerges for the majority of people in government and society at large. Herein lies the power of the people. Ethical nonviolent activists seek to bend the moral arc further so that justice comes sooner rather than later. Judgment is left in the hands of a divine authority while forgiveness is offered as part of the sacrificial life, freeing the believer from both the desire for revenge and the debilitating condition of hate.

---

* Martin Luther King Jr. actually borrowed the image of a moral arc bending toward justice from Theodore Parker (1810-1860), a Unitarian minister and one of the founders of the American Transcendentalist movement. Parker's exact words are as follows: "Look at the facts of the world. You see a continual and progressive triumph of the right. I do not pretend to understand the moral universe; the arc is a long one, my eye reaches but little ways; I cannot calculate the curve and complete the figure by the experience of sight; I can divine it by conscience. And from what I see I am sure it bends towards justice." (Parker, T. "Of Justice and Conscience," in Ten Sermons of Religion. Boston: Crosby, Nichols, & Company, 1853).

One evening an old Cherokee told his grandson about a battle that goes on inside all people. He said, "My son, the battle is between two 'wolves' inside us all. One is Evil. It is anger, envy, jealousy, sorrow, regret, greed, arrogance, self-pity, guilt, resentment, inferiority, lies, false pride, superiority, and ego. The other is Good. It is joy, peace, love, hope, serenity, humility, kindness, benevolence, empathy, generosity, truth, compassion and faith." The grandson thought about it for a minute and then asked his grandfather: "Which wolf wins?" The old Cherokee simply replied, "The one you feed."

—Cherokee legend, author unknown

Chapter 4

Peace, Activism, and the Power of the People

> *If it [the unjust law] is of such a nature that it requires you to be the agent of injustice to another, then, I say, break the law.*
> —Henry David Thoreau,
> *On the Duty of Civil*
> *Disobedience*

As a boy, I recall my fascination with the American Revolution and the Civil War. The sandbox in my elementary-school classroom made it fun to simulate General Pickett's disastrous charge at Gettysburg along with other monumental battles. My classmates and I did so without giving a second thought to the number of soldiers killed or wounded, let alone the wives that were widowed and the children left fatherless.

Reflecting on such childhood memories prompts me to ask: at what age is a person genuinely able to empathize and show compassion? At what point do we recognize that war is not sandbox play or an action video game we can walk away from? When do we fully realize there are deep and lasting social and psychological repercussions to violence? However we decide to answer these questions, one thing is clear: every person must be sensitized to the effects of violence in all its forms, and every generation must be taught effective nonviolent strategies for resolving conflict.

While the history of military conflicts is well documented and dramatized in both print and in movies, educators, until recently, have neglected the struggles waged by activists despite the fact that in America, social activism dates back to colonial times. The First Amendment to the United States

Constitution, which guarantees freedom of speech and religion, freedom of the press, the right to peaceably assemble, and the right to petition the government, laid the groundwork for legitimizing public activism and the social movements that would have a profound impact on American society. It is therefore only fitting that in the twenty-first century, the history and philosophy of nonviolence be placed on an equal footing with military science.

Lessons from History

In the American colonies, peace churches emerged as the first social justice organizations. These congregations included the Mennonites, the Society of Friends or Quakers, the Church of the Brethren, the Amish, Shakers, and the Moravians.* Among the issues addressed by these religious groups were the role of personal conscience, witchcraft, the treatment of Indians, the definition of treason, and the institution of slavery.

The first major issue to present itself in colonial times was known as the Antinomian Controversy. Antinomy refers to a contradiction between two valid laws or conclusions. There was a small group of Puritans who gravitated around the idea that in matters of the spirit, following one's inner light should supersede or overrule theological law and church doctrine. Anne Hutchinson, Mary Dyer, John Cotton, and Roger Williams were among those who propagated this teaching. Because of their beliefs, they were banished from the Massachusetts Bay colony. Later, inspired by the theology of English Quaker George Fox, these individuals would return several times to Massachusetts to promote Fox's teachings, only to be persecuted and tortured. Punishments included flogging, having an ear cropped and, for repeat offenders, having a hole bored through the tongue with a hot iron rod.[1]

When Anne Hutchison was banished from the colony of Massachusetts, she founded the town of Portsmouth. This, along with the towns of Providence (founded by Roger Williams) and Newport, became the colony of Rhode Island. Mary Dyer was warned not to return to the Massachusetts

---

*   The peace churches varied in their pacifist beliefs. The Amish and Mennonites held to absolute pacifism. They would not participate in government but paid their taxes, rendering "to Caesar the things that are Caesar's" (Matt. 22: 20-21). Others, like the Quakers, voted and could hold public office, believing they should be a social force to bring about positive change. As the Civil War approached, the Moravians gave up their pacifism (Jezer, *The Power of the People,* ed. Cooney and Michalowski, 17).

settlement lest she be hanged. She chose nevertheless to challenge the Puritan authority and died on the gallows. Today, a statue in her honor stands outside the Massachusetts State House. Mary Dyer's execution was the culmination of a civil disobedience campaign that eventually gained the attention of King Charles II. After receiving several petitions and hearing testimony, he ordered a halt to the persecution of Quakers by the government of Massachusetts.[2]

The teaching of the supremacy of one's inner light became the central tenet of the Quakers and in time evolved into the issue of "freedom of conscience." Many members of the Society of Friends, which had been established by George Fox and Margaret Fell, left England to flee persecution and were given refuge in Rhode Island. In 1682, Quaker leader William Penn founded the colony of Pennsylvania. Penn declared what became known as the Great Law of Pennsylvania, which guaranteed freedom of conscience to its citizens.[3] Eventually, freedom of conscience, at least within the domain of religious practice, was mandated in the First Amendment of the Bill of Rights of the United States Constitution.

The belief in freedom of conscience provoked debate during the American Revolution over whether refusing to fight the British constituted treason. It also became the battle cry of conscientious objectors who refused to bear arms on religious principle. The Second Amendment to the U.S. Constitution guarantees American citizens the right to bear arms. Given the animosity toward pacifists during times of war, perhaps there should also be an amendment in the U.S. Constitution guaranteeing Americans the right to refuse to bear arms.*

---

* To be a conscientious objector, it has been a requirement of the United States Selective Service agency that a person be opposed to all war. This stipulation, however, does not honor the true meaning of freedom of conscience. Wars can be rooted in very different issues, political circumstances, and have different military goals. One can, in good conscience, adopt a position of relative pacifism where a person is opposed to one war yet is in favor of another. The U.S. role in the Vietnam War was very different than its role in World War II. Similarly, the circumstances leading up to the Second Gulf War with Iraq, for instance, the unsubstantiated claim that Saddam Hussein had weapons of mass destruction, were very different from the first Gulf War launched in response to Iraq's unlawful invasion of Kuwait. The principle of freedom of conscience, therefore, should permit a person to refrain from participating in any given war without requiring adherence to the absolute position of being opposed to all war.

In the early 1800s, there was a departure from church-centered peace activism. Two major secular organizations emerged in the United States, these being the New England Non-Resistance Society, which appealed to the educated elite, and the League of Universal Brotherhood, whose membership consisted mostly of working-class citizens.[4] The dominant issue during this antebellum period was the abolition of slavery, but the women's rights movement also began gathering momentum. This was due primarily to the leadership of Quaker women. Unlike other Christian denominations, the Society of Friends permitted women to speak in church and thereby contribute to unprogrammed Quaker meetings. After the Civil War, Quaker women asserted their freedom of speech and became leaders in the women's rights movement and the struggle for woman's suffrage. Lucretia Mott, Susan B. Anthony, and later, suffragist Alice Paul were leading Quaker women at the forefront of the struggle for women's rights.

The right to vote, however, was not the only issue that fueled the women's rights movement. Americans often forget that the framers of the United States Constitution did nothing to support the rights of women. The domestic rights married women have in the United States today were painfully won by nonviolent activists in the late nineteenth century, well before the suffrage amendment was passed in 1920. Gradually, one by one, individual states passed legislation recognizing a woman's right to own property, inherit their husband's wealth, attend college, draw up a will, and gain custody of their children in cases of divorce.[5]

The most renowned contributor to theories of nonviolent resistance prior to the Civil War was Henry David Thoreau. In addition to his literary masterpiece *Walden*, Thoreau is known for his essay *On the Duty of Civil Disobedience*, which was inspired by a night he spent in jail on July 23, 1846 for refusing to pay his poll tax.

Civil Disobedience was first published in 1849 under the title of "Resistance to Civil Government." The essay was written during a dark time in American history at the height of the slavery controversy. The United States government had been engaged in a war of aggression against Mexico in pursuit of its "manifest destiny." Thoreau maintained there is a higher moral law of conscience which people are obligated to follow even if it conflicted with the laws of the state. If a law forces a person to behave unjustly toward another, he asserted, we are morally obligated to violate the law. When the machinery of government propagates injustice, we must provide resistance, "be a counter friction to stop the machine." Although Thoreau did not actually reject government, anarchists nevertheless herald him for proclaiming in the opening paragraph of his famous essay, "a government's best that governs not at all."

In addition to Thoreau, the influence of Adin Ballou, a Unitarian minister, was also significant.* Ballou promoted what he called "principled pacifism" and authored a book entitled *Christian Non-Resistance.* In it he articulated his concepts of "moral resistance" and "uninjurious, benevolent physical force," such as might be used to restrain or disarm someone who could potentially cause harm to others.[6] Ballou justified the use of physical force as long as it was not *intended* to cause injury.

Outside the United States, Russian author Leo Tolstoy wrote his seminal work on nonviolence, *The Kingdom of God Is Within You*, which confronted church dogma and asserted that "nonresistance to evil by force" was central to Christ's teaching. His earlier work, *What I Believe*, criticized what Tolstoy held was the perversion of Christ's teaching by the church. *What I believe* was subject to Russian censorship but circulated underground and attracted considerable attention. It is known that Tolstoy, and perhaps also Adin Ballou and Henry Thoreau, influenced the person who contributed most to nonviolent theory, this being Mohandas K. Gandhi.

Gandhi's Contribution

Recognized for his successful nonviolent campaigns in South Africa and India, Mahatma Gandhi was a prolific writer who left a legacy of thoughtful commentary on the philosophy of noncooperation and nonviolent resistance.† While history tends to view Gandhi as a grassroots political figure, he is more understandable as a spiritual leader for whom the independence of India was actually a secondary goal. His primary focus was providing a spiritual path for his followers and, more inclusively, the Indian people—Sikhs, Hindu, and Muslim alike. The following quote from *The Way to God* reveals that Gandhi saw service to one's fellow citizens as an important part of the journey to God realization.

> Man's ultimate aim is the realization of God, and all of his activities—social, political, religious—have to be guided by the ultimate aim of the vision of God. The immediate service of human beings becomes a necessary part of the endeavor, simply

---

*   Adin Ballou's cousin, Hosea Ballou, was a leading Universalist minister during the first half of the nineteenth century. Adin Ballou (1803-1890) began as a Universalist minister but later became a Unitarian.

†   The title *Mahatma* means "great soul."

because the only way to find God is to see him in his creation and be one with it. This can only be done through one's country.[7]

Gandhi's emphasis on spiritual development, personal sacrifice, self-reliance, individual discipline, and emotional restraint made him somewhat of an enigma to both his followers and to the British colonizers. In addition, his training as an attorney made him a skilled debater. He was a tough opponent for British politicians.

Gandhi's teaching, however, must be considered more that a spiritual philosophy. It is a fourfold practice that social justice activists should observe. The first practice is *ahimsa*, which is usually translated to mean nonviolence; i.e., to refrain from injuring or causing harm, either physically or psychologically. Expressed in the positive, ahimsa implies preserving and having reverence for life, as well as acting toward one another with compassion and understanding. Reverence for life also means respecting one's own life by maintaining standards of moral discipline and not seeking personal martyrdom. We must strive to live so we can continue our efforts to expose injustice.*

Ahimsa can be practiced both personally and collectively. On a personal level, one applies nonviolence when dealing with conflicts that may arise during daily activity. On a collective level, activist groups organize and take nonviolent action to rectify an unjust policy or social condition that negatively impacts a particular individual or social group.

The Sanskrit word *himsa* denotes acting with intention to cause harm. The prefix *a* as in ahimsa nullifies this meaning but should not be interpreted as an antonym (i.e., having opposite meaning). *Vidya*, for example, in Sanskrit means knowledge, but *avidya* does not mean *not knowing*. Rather, avidya designates ignorance, which is a condition of being unaware that one does not know. The prefix *non* in nonviolence must be understood in a similar context.

Consider, by comparison, the word *nonattachment*. The opposite of attachment is not nonattachment, but *detachment*. Nonattachment means a person is neither attached nor detached. It implies action that is free from desiring a selfish outcome, but it does not mean a person performs action without regard to its effect on others or with a disinterested frame of mind. So too, ahimsa or nonviolence is not the opposite of violence. As Michael Nagler explains, "Ahimsa is not really a negative term, as to our ears,

---

*   Suicide bombers or Buddhist monks who protest by setting themselves on fire violate the practice of ahimsa.

nonviolence decidedly is. Ahimsa suggests something profoundly positive, which would not be possible to name directly."[8]

It is known that Buddha and Aristotle taught paths of moderation. For Buddha, it was the "middle way;" for Aristotle, it was the principle of the mean between two excesses. The teaching of moderation is also found in chapter 6 of the Bhagavad Gita: "Yoga is not for him who eats too much, or does not eat at all. It is not for him . . . who sleeps too much or keeps too much awake." It is rather "for one who is moderate in food and amusement, restrained in the performance of his actions."[9] It is in this context of moderation and restraint that we must interpret ahimsa.*

Violence is one extreme, but nonviolence must not be thought of as the opposite extreme. It is not complacency, inaction, or giving in to corrupt leaders to appease them. Rather, ahimsa denotes constructive and determined action that is undertaken with the aim of revealing the truth. Indeed, Gandhi saw the concepts of ahimsa and truth as virtually inseparable.

The second practice in Gandhi's teaching is called *satyagraha*. Often translated as "soul force," it is also interpreted to mean "truthful effort" or "clinging to the truth." In contemplating the importance of truth, we must recognize the various ways truth can be expressed.

When the word truth is mentioned, many people immediately think of empiricism or how truth is determined using the scientific method. Empirical truth consists of factual or historical knowledge gained through direct observation or by examining physical evidence or verbal testimony.

A second form of truth consists of wise sayings or proverbs that serve as a guide for living. "Love thy neighbor as thyself" or "Honesty is the best policy" are examples of what may be called proverbial truths.

Truth is also expressed in allegories where it is revealed by understanding the meaning of symbols and metaphors found in stories, myths, and parables. In this book, I have interpreted several myths to explore their potential allegorical meaning and the lessons they are intended to teach.

Finally, there is what may be called perceptual truth, or the ability to experience an object "as it is," free from personal prejudice or bias. Henry David Thoreau describes such an experience in chapter 4 of his book, *A Week on the Concord*

---

* Jesus apparently taught moderation as well. The Gospel of Mark indicates that he did not require his disciples to practice austerities as revealed when the people asked him: "Why do [John the Baptist's] disciples and the disciples of the Pharisees fast, but your disciples do not fast?" (Mark 2:18).

and Merrimack Rivers, where he recalls hearing the beating of a drum from afar, to which he and his brother "listened with such an unprejudiced sense as if for the first time we heard at all." The experience is perhaps more commonly understood as perceiving something as a child would for the very first time, coming to the experience from a condition of innocence. Some people might consider this last form of truth impossible to achieve. However, we can, to a significant degree, become aware of the biases we are superimposing onto our experience and then purposefully choose to minimize their influence. This can happen through personal reflection or through dialogue as we subject our experience and conclusions to the criticism of trusted colleagues. In pursuing truth, we must be aware of its multiple forms and not rely solely on its empirical form as many people often do.

In addition to seeking and upholding truth, Gandhi's concept of satyagraha connotes sacrificial action, selfless service, and a willingness to suffer for a just cause by allowing oneself to become a sacrificial victim of an injustice. This practice is intended to call public attention to injustice without striking back or seeking revenge. Proactively, satyagraha initiates struggle and seeks to keep opponents off balance by doing the unexpected.[10] It requires "a kind of strength that does not come from numbers or from weapons."[11] Rosa Parks was publicly arrested and taken to jail when she refused to give up her seat in the front of a bus in Montgomery, Alabama. In doing so, she performed an act of satyagraha. Her sacrifice triggered the Montgomery bus boycott that paralyzed the city and helped expose the rampant racism in the southern United States. Through her quiet courage and civil disobedience, she exemplified what Thoreau referred to as "a majority of one."*

While Gandhi's early writings made use of the phrase "passive resistance," he later came to reject such language.[12] In Gandhi's view, nonviolence applied in the pursuit of social justice is not passive, nor is it submissive or complacent. It involves direct action and is actually a form of fighting. As Michael Nagler emphatically explains, "Satyagraha is not passive," and in the same breath, he adds, "You are not being 'Gandhian' when you are full of hatred but happen—for the moment—to be keeping your finger off the trigger."[13] I therefore characterize satyagraha as assertive nonviolent action that is free from hostile intention.

---

*   "Any man more right than his neighbors constitutes a majority of one" (from *On the Duty of Civil Disobedience* by H. D. Thoreau).

Satyagraha has its greatest impact if we choose an injustice that the public will perceive as beyond compromise. Activists then intentionally allow themselves to become public victims of the injustice while seizing the "high moral ground," refusing to engage in unethical and violent behavior. Through the practice of satyagraha, activists create a groundswell of public support, setting in motion political mechanisms that bring about reform.

It is vital, however, that activists hold fast to the high moral ground as once this moral ground is lost, it is almost impossible to gain it back. We lose the high moral ground by engaging in the very actions we are protesting against or by committing actions judged as morally or ethically irresponsible. Such actions become a distraction to the message central to our cause. For activists to be respected, they must be ethical. From the peace studies perspective, violence is a form of weakness while ethical nonviolent perseverance is a form of strength.

The third practice in Gandhi's philosophy is *tapasya*. This term comes from the Sanskrit word *tapas*, meaning austerity. It is the discipline whereby one conserves or restrains anger. Often our initial autonomic response when thrown into a conflict is to become angry and feel threatened. This gives rise to what is called the "flight or fight response," which is an adaptive defense mechanism humans inherited over millions of years of biological evolution. When we as modern humans allow the fight or flight response to take hold of our behavior, the conflict we are confronting is usually inflamed. Tapasya enables a person to subdue this autonomic defense mechanism so that reason prevails and one does not act irresponsibly out of anger or fear.

Unfortunately, tapasya is often misunderstood as being a condition of anger repression. On the contrary, the power of tapasya is actually *drawn* from a person's anger, which is now seen as a positive force. Theologian Walter Wink, in his book *The Powers That Be*, concisely explains the role anger should play: "[People] need to be energized by their anger. Then they can freely renounce violence for a nonviolent alternative that transforms the energy of their anger into a dynamic and resolute love."[14]

It can be said that tapasya is a practice akin to meditation. When we truthfully acknowledge and prayerfully reflect on our anger, the negative energy generating the anger is soon transformed and rechanneled into positive action that is more likely to succeed. Our energy is then directed not with vengeance toward individuals, but constructively toward issues and unjust systems. During the practice of tapasya, we are temporarily nonresponsive until an epiphany occurs. The epiphany comes as an insight or realization that reveals to us an effective, positive nonviolent response. In this context, nonviolent conflict resolution is not a zero-sum game where one side wins and the other side loses (i.e., + 1 + −1 = 0). Rather, a course is undertaken where both sides gain and reap the benefit of resolving the conflict. From the Gandhian point of view, peace by means of nonviolence is both the goal *and* the path.

The fourth practice central to Gandhi's philosophy is *swaraj*, usually translated to mean "home rule" or "self-rule." Gandhi first introduced this concept in his landmark treatise *Hind Swaraj*, the English translation of which appeared in South Africa in 1910.[15] The title can have a dual meaning since it suggests that both self-mastery and personal discipline through sacrificial action (satyagraha) are the means to successful nonviolent resistance. In *Hind Swaraj*, Gandhi proposed the extensive use of noncooperation on the part of Indian citizens in the form of strikes, boycotts, civil disobedience, and tax resistance that would paralyze the British government. The threat of such radical ideas prompted the British censors to ban the book in India. But it was to no avail. Twenty years later, the world would see the implementation of Gandhi's call for mass civil disobedience initiated by his famous 240-mile march to the sea to make salt.

From a twenty-first-century perspective, the practice of swaraj can be interpreted as applicable to the individual, community, or the nation. On the individual level, swaraj is similar to Ralph Waldo Emerson's call for self-reliance. It implies not being economically dependent on another person so satyagraha in the form of direct sacrificial action can be pursued without fear of economic loss or reprisal. Gandhi recognized, however, that not everyone could participate in civil disobedience. A mother who must care for her children or a father who needs to provide for his family cannot risk the consequence of defying the law and receiving a jail sentence. Such individuals, however, can still take part in legal forms of noncooperation, such as boycotts, marches, publishing, demonstrations, and the signing of petitions.

Applied to the community, swaraj refers to strengthening local economies, preserving cottage industries, and resisting the encroachment of large industries. The infusion of British tanneries and textile mills in Gandhi's time, for example, caused inflation, disrupted local economies, imported dehumanizing production-line jobs, and created resentment in the villages between those who were hired and those rejected. At Gandhi's request, Indian citizens responded by burning their British-made garments and tediously spinning their own cloth.

In the context of foreign policy, the principle of swaraj is often misunderstood to mean isolationism. Self-sufficiency and self-reliance, however, is not isolationism. Rather, it means obtaining and maintaining for oneself a significant degree of economic independence. This does not mean a country cannot engage in productive trade relations. Trade, especially in an age of increasing globalization, is a powerful tool for nation states to build positive peace and develop valued cooperative relationships. What is to be avoided is economic dependence on a particular good such that a nation becomes vulnerable should that product or resource suddenly be disrupted or withdrawn. Economic dependence places a country in a condition where the denial of a traded product could be used as a weapon, and the dependent country feels pressured to go to war to keep the valued product accessible. Adhering to the principle of swaraj prevents such vulnerability from weakening a nation's international status.

As an example, the United States and Europe have placed themselves in a dependent and vulnerable position with their reliance on foreign oil.* President George W. Bush, in his 2007 State of the Union address, even went so far as to say the United States is "addicted to oil." Overdependence on foreign energy is a violation of the Gandhian principle of swaraj, and this dependence continues to weaken the economic stability of Western nations.

Gandhi also was the first to interpret Jesus' teaching "turn the other cheek"[16] not as a doctrine of submission, but as a teaching of nonviolent resistance. Rather than strike back or run, we are to stand our ground and be willing to take multiple blows if necessary to call public attention to the injustice we are enduring. Walter Wink argues in support of this interpretation, explaining that in Roman culture, a man would strike a subordinate, be it his slave, wife, or child, on the right cheek with the back of his right hand to insult, humiliate, and assert dominance. Even today, we use the word *backhanded* to refer to a degrading act or gesture. But if the subordinate turned away, offering the left cheek, the resulting angle is such that the assailant can no longer strike the subordinate's right cheek. "Turning the other cheek" then becomes an act of defiance, a means of standing one's ground while resisting the reprimand.[17] †

The purpose of nonviolent activism then, from a Gandhian perspective, is to resist injustice and make it visible, bringing it to public attention so

---

*   The exception is France, which meets most of its energy needs with nuclear power.

†   Wink also explains how, when Jesus told his subjugated followers to go the extra mile, or offer a person who sues them their cloak as well as their coat, he was actually advocating forms of nonviolent resistance (see *The Powers that Be,* pages 103-111).

the injustice can be addressed before a violent crisis erupts. Through the practice of tapasya, a person defuses personal anger and abstains from violent retaliation. The negative and often irrational emotion of anger is redirected with a positive intention that invariably results in the realization of a far more effective strategy for approaching the conflict. Rather than defeat our adversaries, we seek to win them over, gaining their moral respect as we publicly force them to see their own injustice.

Ultimately, nonviolence aims not merely to expose injustice and resolve conflict, but to achieve reconciliation. As it says in the often-recited 23rd Psalm, "Thou [God] prepares a table before me and my enemies."[18] To reconcile with our enemies, we must gather around the table of negotiation, share a meal, and see our enemies as fellow human beings. While conflict resolution seeks to stop violence and settle disputes, reconciliation strives to reestablish friendships and restore working relationships. Resolution requires tolerance from conflicting parties; reconciliation demands understanding and forgiveness. In the late twentieth century, this move toward reconciliation was best exemplified by South African president Nelson Mandela.

Mandela was a passionate revolutionary in the 1950s who led armed protests against the human rights abuses of the apartheid government in South Africa. He was eventually arrested, convicted of treason against the apartheid government, and spent twenty-seven years in prison. Throughout the 1980s, domestic protests, increased international pressure, and economic sanctions convinced the white South African government to release Mandela, negotiate an end to apartheid, and hold free elections. In 1994, elections were finally held, and the African National Congress and Nelson Mandela emerged to lead the new South Africa.[19]

There remained, however, a serious risk of civil war among competing tribal groups. Rather than seek punishment and vengeance, Mandela chose the path of forgiveness and set an example no one who had suffered less than him could stand against. He used his persuasive influence to establish, along with Archbishop Desmond Tutu, the South African Truth and Reconciliation Commission. By forgiving those who had condemned him as a political prisoner, he convinced South Africans to tell their stories of human rights abuses, then move beyond hostilities to end division and suspicion. As he insisted in his inaugural address, "We must, therefore, act together as a united people, for national reconciliation, for nation building, for the birth of a new world."[20] Mandela's calm and persuasive leadership enabled his country to avoid a bloody civil war. South Africa had been reborn.

Gandhi and the Gita

In his well-researched dual biography of Mahatma Gandhi and Winston Churchill, Arthur Herman mentions the importance of the Bhagavad Gita and its influence on Gandhi. The first two chapters of the Gita tell the story of Lord Krishna lifting Arguna, who is a great archer and warrior, out of his depression. Arjuna is standing in his chariot, despondent as he contemplates the consequences of going to war against members of his extended family. Krishna calls upon Arjuna to fulfill his duty as a warrior and resolve to fight. His argument first establishes the immortality of the soul, then speaks to the importance of fulfilling one's duty according to the social class or caste with which one is affiliated.

> It [the soul] is never born, nor does it die, nor having once been, will it again cease to be. It is unborn, eternal and everlasting. This primeval one is not slain when the body is slain . . . weapons do not cut it, nor fire burn it; waters do not make it wet, nor does wind make it dry. The soul in the body of everyone, O Arjuna, is eternal and indestructible. Therefore thou shouldst not mourn for any creature.[21]

> Furthermore, having regard for thine own dharma [duty], thou shouldst not tremble. There exists no greater good for a Kshatriya [member of the warrior caste] than a battle required by duty. But if thou wilt not wage this righteous battle, then having thrown away thy duty and glory, thou wilt incur sin.[22]

> Besides, men will forever speak of thy dishonor, and for one who has been honored dishonor is worse than death . . . . If thou art slain, thou wilt obtain heaven, or if thou conquer, thou wilt enjoy the earth. Therefore arise . . . and resolve to fight.[23]

Taken out of context from the Bhagavad Gita's remaining sixteen chapters, Lord Krishna's teaching appears to sanction violence if a person undertakes a battle free from doubt and with unfailing commitment. You could even say that these verses, one referring to a "battle required by duty" and another to a promised "heavenly reward," sound like a call to holy war. If the reader proceeds to the Gita's third chapter, however, a much different message is unveiled, making it clear that the actual battle being portrayed here is an internal one. Starting with verse 36 of chapter 3, Arjuna asks Krishna, "Then by what is a man impelled to [commit] sin against his will, as if compelled by force . . . ?" Krishna replies,

> It is desire, it is wrath, born of the guna [quality] of passion, all devouring and very sinful. Know that this is the enemy here. As fire is covered by smoke, as a mirror by dust, and as an embryo is enveloped by the womb, so is knowledge covered by passion. Knowledge is enveloped by this constant enemy of the knower, by this insatiable flame of desire . . . . Having known that which is greater than reason, steady the self by the Self, slay the enemy, O mighty-armed one, that has the form of desire, and that is so hard to approach.[24, *]

What emerges from this discourse is an allegorical inner battle to be waged against either the learned or instinctive reaction to threatening behavior. The Gita calls upon the devotee to resist acting out of passion, anger, and revenge, a discipline encapsulated in Gandhi's concept of *tapasya*. Later, in chapter 17 of the Gita, the teaching of nonviolence, along with the virtues of beneficial speech, tranquility of mind, and self-control, is clearly articulated as Krishna reveals the austerities associated with the body, speech, and mind.

> Paying homage to the gods, to the twice-born, to teachers and the wise; practicing purity, uprightness, chastity, nonviolence, this is called the austerity of the body. Speaking words that cause no excitement, but are truthful, beneficial; and the practice of Vedic study—this is called the austerity of speech. Attaining tranquility of mind, gentleness, silence, self-control, purity of being—this is called the austerity of mind.[25]

This teaching of nonviolence, as it unfolds in the Bhagavad Gita, has prompted Hindu sages to interpret the story of Arjuna and Krishna poised for battle as a call to attain personal self-mastery. In this context, the chariot in which Arjuna and Krishna are standing represents the physical body. Arjuna is each person's individual self or *jiva* while Lord Krishna is the higher

---

*   Like the Gita, the Epistle of James in the Christian scriptures also sees desire as the cause of sin. "But each person is tempted when he is lured and enticed by his own desire. Then desire, when it has conceived, gives birth to sin" (James 1:14-15).

spiritual "Self" or Atman. The horses pulling the chariot represent the senses while the reins in the hands of Arjuna symbolize the intellect, which is the means by which the senses are subdued and controlled.[26, 27]

Arjuna's recognition that when the battle begins he will be slaying his own relatives symbolizes the awareness whereby one realizes the higher Self is the "self of all beings." All people and all things are related and interdependent.

Thus, rather than serve as a justification for war and violent conflict, the Gita is a discourse on self-mastery and the means through which one should engage in sacrificial action on the battlefield of life. Gandhi applies this teaching to social justice, asserting that it is possible to "fight" using nonviolence. For Gandhi, this is satyagraha, "soul force," and the Mahatma envisioned training an army of nonviolent warriors that could put satyagraha into practice and ultimately end humanity's obsession with war.

Tibet and the Dalai Lama

In 1949, renowned American writer and broadcaster Lowell Thomas began dreaming of a trip to the remote country of Tibet. In addition to opening the eyes of the West to this land at the "top of the world," he was hoping to meet Tenzin Gyatso, the fourteenth Dalai Lama and spiritual leader of what at the time was the world's only theocracy. It was a dream he never thought would materialize, having heard from Leroy W. Henderson, the American ambassador to India, that "the doors of Tibet remained closed as ever."[28] To his surprise and exuberance, Thomas received a midnight call in July 1949, informing him that his request had been approved. He had asked that four other Americans, including his son Lowell Jr., accompany him on the journey, but only his son was approved.

After a long and strenuous trek through treacherous Himalayan mountain passes carrying photographic and recording equipment on horses and mules, Thomas, his son, and their Tibetan guides and translator spent over a week in the city of Lhasa. There they were received by the Dalai Lama and even gained permission to photograph the spiritual leader.

On the return trip, Lowell Thomas Sr. was thrown by his horse, causing him to fall onto the rocks over the trail's edge. At seventeen thousand feet, he had broken his hip in eight places and was now in extreme pain. Thomas credits his son, Lowell Jr., "without whose resourcefulness and determination to get me out alive I could have never made it," with saving his life.[29] He was the one American the Dalai Lama approved to accompany Thomas Sr. to Lhasa.

Lowell Thomas and his son speculated that the reason for this reception by the Dalai Lama was the pressing threat of Chinese communist forces who were winning the civil war against Chiang Kai-shek. Shortly after Thomas and his caravan left Tibet, the Chinese overran the country and forced Tibetan monks out of their monasteries. The expedition of Lowell Thomas and his son into Tibet and the subsequent publicity it brought to Tibetan culture is another example of the important role media can play in exposing injustice.

In the 1950s, what is known historically as the Cultural Revolution swept through China. Mao Tse-tung and his communist cohorts began pressuring the people of Tibet to become part of the "motherland." What began as a political incursion soon became a ruthless campaign to destroy Tibetan culture and oppress the Tibetan people. After a failed revolt in 1959, the Dalai Lama fled his native land, taking refuge in Dharamsala, India, where he now presides over his government in exile.

Since his escape, the Tibetan leader has been the figurehead of a nonviolent movement to familiarize the west with Tibetan Buddhism and restore cultural autonomy to Tibet. Although Chinese leaders insist the Dalai Lama is a separatist seeking independence for his country, the Tibetan leader has repeatedly denied this, insisting he seeks only genuine cultural autonomy; that is, the right of the Tibetan people to practice their form of Buddhism, preserve their ancient traditions, and manage their own cultural affairs.

The Dalai Lama's adherence to nonviolence and his nonattachment to political outcomes continue to expose the oppressive policies of Chinese government leaders. He has gained the support of Western nations, and his efforts have generated a sustained interest in Tibetan Buddhism and Tibetan culture. Several full-length movies focusing on the Tibetan struggle have enjoyed great popularity. Major Tibetan cultural centers have been established in the West; among them are centers in Toronto, Indianapolis, and in Bloomington, Indiana. In 1989, the Dalai Lama was awarded the Nobel Peace Prize, and he subsequently has published several successful books elaborating on Buddhist philosophy. Other Tibetan monks, such as Sakyong Mipham with his book *Ruling Your World*,* have also contributed to the literature explaining Tibetan Buddhist teachings. These achievements illustrate what Walter Wink refers to as the gifts of the enemy[30] that are won

---

*   Sakyong Mipham, *Ruling Your World: Ancient Strategies for Modern Life.* (New York: Morgan Road Books, 2005).

Lucretia Mont (1793-1880)

Susan B. Anthony (1820-1906)

Adin Ballou (1803-1890)

Henry David Thoreau (1817-1862)

Leo Tolstoy (1828-1910)

Alice Paul (1885-1977)

Mohandas K. (Mahatma) Gandhi (1869-1948)

A. J. Muste (1885-1967)

Eugene Debs (1855-1926)

Dorothy Day (1897-1980)

Peter Maurin (1877-1949)

Upton Sinclair (1878-1968)

Rev. Dr. Martin Luther king Jr. (1929-1968)

Cesar Chavez (1927-1993)

Harvey Milk (1930-1978)

Nelson Mandela (b. 1918)

Tenzin Gyatso, the fourteenth Dalai Lama (b. 1935)

Archbishop Desmond Tutu (b. October 1931)

Lech Wałęsa (b. 1943)

R. Buckminster Fuller (1895-1983)

through the restraint of anger and the openness to opportunities that lie outside the imprisoning psychological boundaries of a conflict.

Critics of the Dalai Lama assert that Tibetan culture and the land ruled by the Lamas for over 550 years has been hopelessly romanticized, that Tibet, before the Chinese began their occupation, was an impoverished and backward nation. They claim the Lamas governed more as tyrants and lived in opulent wealth at the expense of lower-class farmers and herders. But such political-economic conditions should not be confused with or blamed on Tibetan religion or its cultural tradition.

Tibet is a landlocked country that until the 1960s was accessible only by those willing to make long and arduous excursions on horses, yaks, and mules through Himalayan mountain passes at elevations well over twelve thousand feet. Rather than a nation isolated by its religion, Tibetan Buddhism and culture was a religion adapted to the rugged geographical isolation of the land. A philosophy of self-reliance gripped the culture out of necessity, influenced certainly by neighboring Hindu culture and its preoccupation with the inner spiritual life. And Tibet's self-sufficiency was undoubtedly reinforced by China's intermittent periods of historical isolation that date back to the Ming Dynasty and the construction of the Great Wall.

The Dalai Lama does not object to China's effort to modernize the country and provide accessible rail and air transportation into Tibet. What he objects to is not having a voice in these development projects. Today, Tibetan monks in India and in the West readily use computer and cellular technology. The Chinese certainly could have gradually introduced these technological advancements without persecuting the Tibetan people, undermining their culture, and suppressing religious practice.

The Dalai Lama's sustained nonviolent effort to restore cultural autonomy to his homeland is an excellent example of how restraining anger broadens an activist's domain of influence and brings unanticipated rewards. His struggle, however, also reveals some of the same problems with discipline among his followers that Gandhi experienced in India. In the months prior to the 2008 summer Olympics that were held in China, Tibetan monks peacefully protested the Chinese occupation of their county. Some of the lay citizens, however, when provoked by the police, began attacking Chinese shops and their owners residing in Tibet. The resulting violence, while understandable given the brutality of the oppression, nevertheless provides the Chinese government an excuse to justify their propaganda characterizing the Dalai Lama as an underhanded separatist. This is the cost of relinquishing the high moral ground.

We can learn a great deal from the example of the fourteenth Dalai Lama, whether we are activist leaders or supporters of a social cause. His is a remarkable story of consistent moral strength, forgiveness, and perseverance.

Misconceptions of Nonviolence

While many people laud the principle of nonviolence, popular belief holds that nonviolence cannot succeed if one of the parties involved in the conflict chooses to use violence. This view is incorrect and reflects an all too common misconception.

Martin Luther King Jr. and his followers during the civil rights movement advocated strict adherence to nonviolence. Yet they were often attacked by police using dogs and fire hoses. The Freedom Riders, when traveling from northern states into the south, intentionally violated the segregation laws at bus terminals. Their buses were bombed and burned. Many black citizens were subject to lynching by the Ku Klux Klan, and several white activists were killed in drive-by shootings. Rosa Parks and others were jailed, and King had his house firebombed. In the women's rights movement, Alice Paul and other activists were arrested, persecuted, and imprisoned in their efforts to secure the passage of the suffrage amendment. The British didn't play by nonviolent rules either, particularly when General Reginald Dyer massacred hundreds of Indian civilians at Amritsar (see page 45). Yet all three of these nonviolent movements succeeded in exposing injustice and instigating reforms with far less loss of life and financial cost than would have resulted from a violent revolution.

Another misconception regarding nonviolent activism is that military action and nonviolence are incompatible and cannot coexist. There are, in fact, times when social justice activists and the military find themselves fighting the same enemy.

Nonviolence works best where national governmental institutions are capable of responding to the injustice being addressed by activists. This was the political environment in America in the 1960s during the civil rights era and in the first half of the twentieth century during the labor movement. But when the political environment is not responsive or during times of war, nonviolence often takes the form of noncooperation and underground movements that work to subvert the power structure, which the military may be called upon to fight.

Before and during World War II, the Dutch Resistance Movement stymied Nazi efforts to round up Jewish citizens living in the Netherlands. The Danes began wearing the identifying Star of David symbol to confuse Nazi authorities. Their efforts also included hiding Jews in private homes and ferrying them to Sweden where many were given refuge. In France, an underground movement worked to hide Jewish families and children separated from their parents.

A personal friend of mine from New York City, Judith Steel, survived the Nazi Holocaust as a child because a French Roman Catholic family gave her refuge in their home despite great personal risk to themselves. Disguised as a little French girl, she was told not to speak to soldiers during the German occupation for fear her accent would reveal her Jewish identity.

Is nonviolence always successful? No, but neither is violence or military action always successful. Violence may succeed in forcing reform, but it rarely results in reconciliation and often sows the seeds for future violent conflict. As Martin Luther King Jr. concisely expressed it, "The aftermath of nonviolence is the creation of the beloved community, while the aftermath of violence is tragic bitterness."

Successes and the Price of Failure

By exercising their First Amendment freedoms, American activists have made the United States an innovator in the theory and practice of nonviolence. In addition to domestic rights for women, the passage of the Nineteenth Amendment granting women the right to vote (see page 64), and the civil rights legislation of the 1960s (see pages 35-36), there are several other successful reforms that must be mentioned. Americans should be proud of the inspiring nonviolent movements that have taken place on their soil.

In the late nineteenth and early twentieth centuries, the working conditions in U.S. and European factories were horrendous. There were no labor laws to prevent employers from exploiting workers to increase their capitalist "bottom line." In response, a dynamic socialist movement took root that was inspired by the economic and political theories of Friedrich Engels and Karl Marx, authors of *The Communist Manifesto*. In 1906, a novel entitled *The Jungle* by Upton Sinclair drew public attention to the corruption in the U.S. meat-packing industry and the plight of immigrant workers in general.* Sinclair was dubbed the original "muckraker," a term

---

*   As often happens in social movements, a secondary issue frequently raises the public ire and provokes reform. In the case of the meat-packing industry, the public outrage regarding meat safety initially trumped the concern over labor practices. Upton Sinclair later complained, "I aimed at the public's heart, and by accident I hit it in the stomach" (www.capitalcentury.com/1906.html).

coined for him by President Theodore Roosevelt. In 1917, the October Bolshevik Revolution overthrew the Russian Czar. These events strengthened the International labor movement that had emerged in the middle-to-late 1800s.

The Labor movement in the United States was shaped by such activists as A. J. Muste,* Eugene Debs, and Norman Thomas who called for the use of nonviolent strategies of direct action rather than Bolshevik-style armed uprisings. By organizing unions and calling for labor strikes, they succeeded in winning the forty-hour workweek, the right to overtime pay, workman's injury compensation, the prohibition of child labor, and federal oversight of the food industry.[31]

It was also through the power of nonviolence that the United Farm Workers led by Cesar Chavez inspired what became a worldwide boycott of California grapes. Their efforts, which included a well-publicized march to the statehouse in Sacramento, won migrant workers in California higher wages, better working conditions, and the right to form a union.[32]

Public opposition to the United States involvement in Vietnam, the military draft, and the twenty-one-year-old voting age in the United States fueled demonstrations during the Vietnam War. Many young men being conscripted into the army to fight in Vietnam were eighteen to twenty years old. They were therefore forced to support U.S. government policy while being denied the right to vote. The year 1971 saw the ratification of the Twenty-sixth Amendment lowering the voting age to eighteen. Vietnam activism also exposed the draft in the 1960s as racially biased. Far more Afro-Americans were being drafted since white Americans were financially in a better position to attend college and thereby have their military service deferred. A lottery system was instituted in 1970, but ultimately, the United States Congress was pressured to end the military draft by 1973 and establish the all-volunteer army.

In San Francisco, activist Harvey Milk generated grassroots support for gay rights in the 1970s. After several unsuccessful runs for public office, Milk was elected in 1977 to serve on the San Francisco Board of Supervisors. He succeeded in having the board pass a landmark gay-rights ordinance in

---

*   Abraham Johannes Muste (1885-1967) was a Dutch reform minister who was ousted
     from his pulpit because of his opposition to World War I. He had a long career as a
     pacifist and was active in the U.S. Labor and civil rights movements. He also served
     as executive director of the Fellowship of Reconciliation from 1940-1953.

1977. His career, however, ended tragically on November 27, 1978, when a disgruntled city supervisor named Dan White assassinated him and George Moscone, the San Francisco mayor.

The nuclear arms race between the United States and the Soviet Union, and the increasing size and power of their nuclear arsenals, became the focus of a wide range of protests during the cold war era. It became known that both superpowers had deployed enough nuclear weapons to destroy each other ten times over. Referred to in military lingo as *overkill,* public momentum was created for a moratorium or *freeze* to halt the testing, production, and deployment of more weapons and for the United States and USSR to reduce their arsenals.[33] Demonstrators gathered at nuclear production facilities and testing grounds, protesting the insanity behind military strategies based on the belief that a nuclear war was survivable. Moreover, there was the very real possibility that a nuclear exchange could occur by accident due to a false alarm.

In an all-out nuclear attack, the missiles, once launched, would reach their target in as little as a half an hour. This creates the necessity for the defending country to respond within thirty minutes or risk losing the ability to launch a retaliatory strike. The danger with this defensive strategy, which is referred to as *launch on warning,* lies in the possibility of a false alarm triggering a nuclear war. The nation that believed it was under attack could be prone to launch prematurely if it misread a radar screen or miscalculated the reading on a satellite sensor. The Senate Armed Services Committee determined there were 151 serious false alarms during an eighteen-month period beginning in January 1979.[34]

Activists further raised public awareness of the tremendous cost of production and deployment of atomic weapons and the resulting diversion of funds from humanitarian causes to support weapons programs. Noted scientists such as Carl Sagan also documented the potential for a "nuclear winter" should a nuclear war occur.

Many people believe nonviolence cannot succeed against authoritarian governments, but the success of the Solidarity movement in communist Poland proves otherwise. Solidarity began in August of 1980 with a massive labor strike at the Gdansk shipyard in the port city of Gdansk. Support for the strike, which was led by electrician Lech Walesa, spread among factory workers until those striking numbered seventeen thousand. After seventeen days, negotiations with Mieczyslaw Jagielski, the deputy prime minister, resulted in the legalization of Solidarity as an independent trade union. The Polish government, however, under pressure from the Soviet Union, soon rescinded the accord. This was a great irony since the foundation of the Soviet Union, with its logo of the hammer and sickle, was rooted in the rise of the working-class proletariat.

Lech Walesa was arrested along with other Solidarity leaders and spent close to a year in prison. In 1983, he was awarded the Nobel Peace Prize for his nonviolent efforts. Meanwhile, Solidarity had gone underground, holding meetings in private residences to continue educating workers to its cause. Support came from American labor unions and from Pope John Paul II, who was a Polish native. In the late 1980s, mass public demonstrations reoccurred, and labor strikes forced the Polish government to recognize Solidarity as an organization rivaling the Communist Party. Elections were subsequently held in June 1989. Solidarity emerged holding the maximum allowable number of parliamentary seats in both houses, and Poland became the first communist bloc nation to embrace democracy.[35]

Despite the success of nonviolence in different parts of the world and under various political systems, there also have been times when government officials did not heed the voice of activists, the consequences of which were disastrous.

From colonial times until the close of the U.S. Civil War, abolitionists worked tirelessly using various forms of direct action, which included sit-ins and the boycott of slave-made goods, to bring an end to the institution of slavery in the United States. Many stores in the north intentionally carried only items produced by free labor. In the late 1700s, pressure brought by anti-slavery organizations, the first of which was started by the Society of Friends, resulted in the northern states passing emancipation laws.

Before and during the Civil War, the Underground Railroad covertly aided slaves in their journey north to freedom. In the early 1800s, prominent U.S. statesmen, including economist Daniel Raymond and former presidents John Quincy Adams and James Madison, wrote letters, journal entries, and articles condemning slavery while discussing ways to wean the southern states off their dependence on a slave-based economy.[36] By 1845, slavery had been abolished in most of Europe as well as in Mexico, Chile, Uruguay, and Bolivia. But in the United States, the slaveholding states and politicians held too much influence. The moral, political, and economic will was simply not present to alter the course of history. The result was a divided nation, the secession of eleven southern states, and a devastating mid-century civil war.

In 1933, Rabbi Steven Wise collaborated with Unitarian minister Rev. John Hayes Holmes. They organized a march in New York City protesting the U.S. State Department's immigration quotas that were preventing large numbers of European Jews from entering the United States to escape the growing hostile anti-Semitism in Nazi Germany. They soon would be joined by Roman Catholic activists Dorothy Day and Peter Maurin. Together they petitioned President Roosevelt and the State Department to change the immigration standards, but the old quotas were left in place.[37] That was six years before the start of World War II and eight years before the Nazi death camps.

In 1939, the ill-fated ocean liner *St. Louis* set sail, carrying over nine hundred European Jews seeking entry into Cuba, the United States, or Canada. The U.S. State Department turned the boat away, leaving the *St. Louis* no choice but to return to Europe. Most of its passengers were eventually taken to Nazi death camps where they perished. Had the United States government responded in 1933 and opened wider its doors, thousands of Jews could have been saved.

In 1964, pacifist leader A. J. Muste teamed up with activist David McReynolds and issued their infamous "Memo on Vietnam" distributed by the War Resisters League. It offered a stinging critique of the United States government's policy toward the growing conflict in Vietnam, boldly stating that a military victory would be next to impossible for the United States to achieve.[38] But the moral and political will was not there to alter the course of history. United States military involvement in Vietnam would escalate without a declaration of war and continue until 1975. Over 55,000 American soldiers and well over 500,000 Vietnamese soldiers lost their lives.

The above examples attest to the devastating consequences that can result when nonviolent leaders and their respective social movements are ignored. Thus, we should listen to our nonviolent activists, for they are the prophets of their time. It is they who bring the Promethean fire to expose injustice, but tragically, it is too often an injustice we do not want to see.

How We Partition History

Historian Dominick LaCapra of Cornell University points out that humans have a habit of partitioning history with violent events.[39] We speak of periods before and after a particular war, such as the antebellum period in U.S. history before the civil war. The "atomic age" is marked not by the splitting of the atom as much as it is by the use of nuclear weapons on Japan, and we now repeatedly hear references to our pre- and post-9/11 world. We have allowed the terrorists to define our age. I personally long for a time when we would instead partition history using great human peacetime achievements, such as the discovery of the polio vaccine or the Apollo moon landing.

What we learn from the remarkable history of nonviolence is that people who are well organized and committed to nonviolence can make a huge difference in the fight against injustice. The truth that exposes injustice and makes it visible to the world is not something we should simply believe in. We must experience and give witness to it. The spirit that energizes nonviolent reform movements must propel us to take selfless action in pursuit of human rights and individual dignity. This experience has absolutely nothing to do with a person's religious affiliation. It matters little whether you are Hindu, Christian, Buddhist, Jewish, Muslim, Baha'i, Native American, atheist, or agnostic. What matters is that you speak truth to power at great risk to your personal reputation and well-being, that you experience the hate in the world firsthand and, after facing it directly, rise to disarm it with understanding, persistence, and unwavering courage.

We cannot have peace if we are only concerned with peace. War is not an accident. It is the logical outcome of a certain way of life. If we want to attack war, we have to attack that way of life.

—A. J. Muste

Chapter 5

Taoism, Fatherhood, and the Martial Arts

There is a saying among soldiers:
  I dare not make the first move but would rather play the guest;
  I dare not advance an inch but would rather withdraw a foot.
This is called marching without appearing to move,
Rolling up your sleeves without showing your arm,
Capturing the enemy without attacking,
Being armed without weapons.

—Tao Te Ching (ch. 79)

Since my days in graduate school, I have been intrigued with the ancient philosophical tradition known as Taoism. My fascination stems from recognizing how the teachings of Taoist philosophy resonate with those of my Christian upbringing. Not until I became involved in peace education, however, did I consider what application Taoist teachings might have to social activism and conflict resolution.

Taoism is said to have originated with the obscure Chinese philosopher Lao-tzu who lived in the sixth century BCE. The Chinese word *Tao* (pronounced "dow") literally means "way." Lao-tzu resided in the province of Honan and was curator of the imperial archives at Loyang. Legend has it that he was asked to write down his teaching of the eternal Tao before departing to spend his last days in the desert.[1] The result was the primary scripture of Taoism, an eloquent text known as the Tao Te Ching.

The opening lines of the Tao Te Ching state the obvious that is too often forgotten; that which gave rise to the universe is ineffable.

The Tao that can be told is not the eternal Tao.
The Name that can be named is not the eternal name.
The nameless is the beginning of heaven and earth.[2]

Existing before language, the beginning of creation is beyond name. Formless and intangible, it is boundless and indefinable. Yet the entire universe in all its wondrous order and diversity came forth from that incomprehensible source, and it is to this nameless and indefinable oneness that all things ultimately return. To experience that oneness in meditation, a person must let go of expectations and all that is assumed to be real. This "letting go" is essential to the process of forgiveness and reconciliation.

Taoism eventually merged with Buddhism as followers of the Buddha migrated northward into China from India. The Tao Te Ching, however, was written perhaps as many as 10 centuries before Buddhist teachings arrived in China. Thus, none of its chapters refer to Buddha's Four Noble Truths or to his Eightfold Path.

Initially, Taoism coexisted with Confucianism. The philosopher Confucius developed a complex system of thought that placed emphasis on social order and the perfectibility of the individual through moral education and training. Taoism, on the other hand, sees such knowledge and training as academic and a potential distraction to spiritual growth. Its focus instead is on spiritual enlightenment, the path to which, according to Lao-tzu, involves cultivating the intuitive, feminine side of human nature.

Compared to other scriptures, the Tao Te Ching is unique in its frequent use of maternal images. In chapter 6 it says, "The valley spirit never dies. It is woman, primal Mother."[3] The valley expresses the quality of fertility but also that which is lowly and humble. Chapter 22 makes use of what is generally stereotyped in Western cultures as feminine characteristics: "Yield and overcome; bend and be straight; empty and be full."[4] Such advice runs counter to the assertive stereotypical masculine approach to problem solving and resolving conflicts.* Furthermore, in chapters 25 and 52, it is not God

---

*   Here masculine and feminine traits are being presented as social constructs although evolutionary psychologists do provide an argument for survival advantage based on characteristics we speak of today as stereotypes. Women, for example, evolved nurturing social roles due to the nine-month human gestation period and the need to nurse infants. Men evolved to be physically stronger and aggressive as it was an advantage in protecting the women and children and in hunting for game.

the Father who brings forth Creation; it is the mysterious maternal power of the universe that gives rise to multiplicity as symbolized by the phrase "ten thousand things."

> Something mysteriously formed,
> Born before heaven and earth,
> In the silence and the void,
> Standing alone and unchanging,
> Ever present and in motion.
> Perhaps it is the mother of ten thousand things.
> I do not know its name.
> Call it Tao.
> For lack of a better word, I call it great.[5]

> The beginning of the universe
> Is the mother of all things.[6]

As introduced in chapter 2, many of the principles expressed in Taoism are paradoxical and invert the worldly value system we so readily accept. Consider, for example, this passage from chapter 7 of the Tao Te Ching: "The sage stays behind, thus he is ahead. He is detached, thus one with all. Through selfless action, he attains fulfillment."

This theme of value inversion is present in Christian scripture in the following verse from the Gospel of Luke where Jesus is quoted as saying, "For everyone who exalts himself will be humbled, and he who humbles himself will be exalted."[7] Jesus also taught that in the Kingdom of God, "Many who are last will be first, and the first, last."[8] The Christian nativity story allegorically dramatizes these teachings. In the Gospel of Luke, for example, who are the people chosen to receive the announcement of Christ's birth? Not the kings or the powerful military leaders; not the legal experts or the educated philosophers of the day. Surprisingly, those privileged to hear the birth announcement are the shepherds, who were of a much lower social status. And the Christ child is born, not in the midst of royalty and wealth where one might expect divinity to reside, but to a poor family living in very humble circumstances.

In addition, Jesus spoke like a Taoist when he told his disciples to become like a child again,[9] a passage reminiscent of chapter 28 in the Tao Te Ching where it says, "Ever true and unswerving, become as a little child once more."[10]

Taoism's compatibility with Buddhism is also found in the value placed on emptiness in the Tao Te Ching. As it says in chapter 4, "The Tao is an empty vessel; it is used but never filled."[11] And again in chapter 11,

> Thirty spokes share the wheel's hub;
> It is the center hole that makes it useful.
> Shape clay into a vessel;
> It is the space within that makes it useful.[12]

From the Taoist (and also Buddhist) perspective, usefulness, purpose, meaning, and essence are found in emptiness. What is not there is more important that what is there. We must, therefore, become empty if we wish to gain enlightenment. We must rid ourselves of ego attachment, prior assumptions, and the desire to control outcomes if we are to become one with the Tao and live in harmony with this natural unfolding process called life.

This metaphor of emptiness is also present in a lesser-known parable attributed to Jesus that is found in the Gospel of Thomas. In verse 97, Jesus likens the kingdom of heaven to a woman whose grain spills by accident from a vessel as a result of a broken handle, leaving her to discover emptiness.

> The Kingdom of the [Father] is like a woman who was carrying
> a [jar] full of meal. While she was walking along [a] distant road,
> the handle of the jar broke and the meal spilled behind her [along]
> the road. She did not know it; she noticed no accident. When she
> reached her house, she put the jar down and discovered that it was
> empty (text adapted by Elaine Pagels and Marvin Meyer).[13]

The handle on a jar is that to which a person latches hold. The breaking of the handle may be said to represent letting go of attachment. Like the meal spilling from the jar, we must pour ourselves spontaneously and fully into life to discover emptiness. Through emptying oneself, life becomes driven by purpose and filled with meaning. In emptiness is found one's essential nature, which is nonphysical and beyond the boundaries of thought.*

---

*   Transcendence in meditation is an experience where the boundaries of thought have completely dissolved. One rests in unbounded bliss and realizes that infinity is both empty and full—empty in the sense that there is no object in the awareness,

That the figure in this parable is a woman and that her discovery of the lost meal occurs by accident speaks to the unplanned, spontaneous way the kingdom of heaven is revealed. It takes a feminine perspective to recognize the accident and the emptiness as profoundly significant. A stereotypical masculine, practical assessment of the event would see it as little more than a careless mistake.*

Several years ago, I was a member of a Sunday-school class at a mainstream protestant church. On Mother's Day, the class leader decided to have each person in the class share personal reflections about their mother. This discussion turned out to be enjoyable and highly meaningful.

A month later, the same class leader decided to engage in a similar discussion about fathers. To everyone's surprise, there was noticeable hesitation as we waited for one of us to begin the sharing of memories. After considerable silence, one person said he never knew his father very well because he was frequently away on business. Another commented on the psychological distance between himself and his dad. I mentioned how my father did not adjust well to retirement and subsequently suffered from depression. He had been the principal of the high school I attended and would awaken me early each morning to take me to school. Like many men of his generation, his expression of love was reserved, conveyed with a firm handshake rather than a hug. In the end, all of us in the Sunday-school class realized how difficult it was to reflect on the relationship each of us had with his or her father. Later that day, I asked myself, why was this pain of separation and relational distance so apparent during our Father's Day discussion? Such apprehension had been virtually absent during the class on Mother's Day.

Psychologists give rather complex explanations for tensions that often exist between children and their fathers. Sigmund Freud attributed competitive hostilities between father and son to the Oedipus complex. Others suggest that a person feels innately closer to one's mother because it is the mother who carries the child in her womb. There are also those who maintain

---

full in the sense that infinity embraces and includes everything. In the experience of transcendence, emptiness and fullness become one.

*   Consistent with the female role in this parable is belief that, after Jesus' crucifixion, according to the Gospel of Matthew, it was two women, one of whom was Mary Magdalene, who found his tomb empty (Matt. 28:1). It is in emptiness that we find new life.

the relational distance experienced between father and child is due to our patriarchal culture, which traditionally sees the father as breadwinner and disciplinarian and the mother as nurturing homemaker. These stereotypical roles are often reinforced by deeply ingrained religious beliefs.

Regardless of the explanation you prefer, it is a common experience that the child-father relationship is often more distant and reserved than the relationship between child and mother. This distance may result in conflict between father and child that follows a person into adulthood. In my case, it was disagreement over long-term goals, managing money, planning for the future, and advancing my career. As we shall see later, applying the maternal principles expressed in Taoist philosophy can help heal the conflicts that emerge from the relational distance between father and child.

Yin and Yang

The primary symbol of Taoism is known as the yin-yang (figure 3). This symbol depicts complementary opposite values coexisting in a condition of mutual give-and-take. People in Western cultures frequently

Figure 3	Figure 4	Figure 5
Yin and yang	Yin and yang redrawn	Yin and yang redrawn
Represents harmony and cooperation	Represents gridlock and an unwillingness to compromise	Represents physical, psychological, and structural violence

ascribe good and evil to the white and black sides of this image, but such values are not part of the Taoist interpretation. Rather, the yin or black side represents mystery, intuition, and the female principle while the yang or white portion symbolizes clarity, intellect, and the stereotypical masculine side of life. The large dots of opposing color in each side of the symbol reveal that the complementary opposites are inseparable and are forever interdependent. This prevents the Taoist duality from being interpreted and applied simplistically. According to the Tao Te Ching, one is to "keep the strength of a man, but keep a woman's care."[14] One must therefore learn to balance the yin and the yang within oneself and facilitate their complimentary flow in creation.

When lecturing on peace education, I often redraw this symbol to represent different kinds of interactions between people. Figure 4 represents an uncompromising condition where interacting parties or individuals have dug in their heels and are unwilling to bend from their respective positions. When this happens in government, we call it gridlock. Figure 5 depicts opposing sides or forces in a state of violence. This jagged yin-yang not only repesents physical violence. It also refers to psychological violence as exhibited in acts of intimidation, harassment, bullying and verbal abuse, and to structural violence which takes the form of oppression and discrimination.

In our patriarchal culture, men are expected, and perhaps conditioned, to be strong, assertive, somewhat intimidating and unyielding as depicted in figure 4. A man who empathizes with his adversaries, who is flexible and willing to compromise as represented in figure 3, is often seen as weak and lacking in leadership ability. This assertive expectation of masculinity undoubtedly contributes to the relational distance experienced between a father and his children. Given that assertiveness and intimidation can easily lead to violent confrontation, it may also help explain why more men engage in violent crime than women.

As previously explained, Taoist teachings, like Zen Buddhist philosophy and the life and teachings of Jesus, are laden with paradoxes.* One of the most surprising is that Taoism, with its emphasis on harmony, humility, yielding to overcome, and seeking to cultivate the feminine side of human nature, is the philosophy out of which the oriental systems of martial arts were born. Many are those who have asked how a martial component could coexist with Taoism. Three explanations can be given for this paradox.

First, in ancient China the sociopolitical system was highly feudal, particularly toward the end of the Zhou Dynasty when Taoism as well as

---

* Zen Buddhism is well known for its puzzling koans which often take the form of paradoxical riddles meant to disengage the disciple's intellect. Many of Jesus' sayings are reminiscent of koans, the most striking being the verse in the ninth chapter of the Gospel of John where he says, "I came into this world, that those who do not see may see, and those who see might be made blind" (John 9:39).

Confucianism began to flourish.* Self-defense was undoubtedly seen as a necessity as territorial lords competed for land and power. Later, with the influence of Buddhism from India, monastic communities emerged around the 6th century CE and became training centers for Shaolin warrior monks. The Taoist yin and yang principle became the basis for hard and soft martial arts techniques.[15] These techniques, however, were not based so much on offensive or aggressive tactics, but instead, focused on learning to take the hostile energy being encountered and turning it against one's opponent. The result is an approach to self-defense which applies the paradoxical teachings found in Taoism. One literally learns the value of "yielding" to overcome an aggressor as is taught in the following verses in the Tao Te Ching:

> Under heaven nothing is more soft and yielding than water,
> Yet for attacking the solid and strong, nothing is better;
> It has no equal.
> The weak can overcome the strong;
> The supple can overcome the stiff.[16]

> The softest thing in the universe
> Overcomes the hardest thing in the universe.
> That without substance can enter where there is no room.[17]

> A leaf, when young is supple and soft, in death it is brittle and
>   breaks.
> A tree, when young bends with the wind, when it is old, it is
>   hard and stiff.
> Therefore hard and stiff is the disciple of death,
> Bending and yielding is the disciple of life.[18]

The second explanation for how the martial arts could coexist with Taoism is that violence in Taoist philosophy is defined by a person's inner mental and emotional state rather than by one's outer behavior. As one Taoist saying expresses it, "For the heart that is one with nature, though the body contend, there is no violence. But for the heart that is not one with nature, though the body be at rest, there is always violence." Violence, like

---

* Historians date the Zhou Dynasty from 1122-256 BCE. Lao-tzu, the author of the *Tao Te Ching*, lived during the sixth century BCE.

harmony, is thus understood to be an internal psychological condition. To shift into a mode of self-defense does not constitute violence if one's heart is free from anger.

In rare instances where Lao-tzu condones combat, he speaks of it with great reservation.

> Good weapons are instruments of fear; all creatures hate them.
> Therefore followers of Tao never use them.
> The wise man prefers the left.
> The man of war prefers the right.

> Weapons are instruments of fear; they are not a wise man's
>   tools.
> He uses them only when he has no choice.
> Peace and quiet are dear to his heart,
> And victory no cause for rejoicing.
> If you rejoice in victory, then you delight in killing;
> If you delight in killing, you cannot fulfill yourself.[19]

In contrast to the patriotic enthusiasm that is often exhibited by the public when soldiers march off to war or return from battle, the Tao Te Ching likens victory in war to a funeral.

> When many people are being killed,
> They should be mourned in heartfelt sorrow.
> That is why a victory must be observed like a funeral.[20]

A third explanation for the coexistence of Taoism and the martial arts is that the martial training that one received in Taoist temples was seen as a metaphor for removing conflict from within oneself. An inner struggle was waged to overcome anger, revenge, impatience, passion, envy, and hatred.

> A good soldier is not violent.
> A good fighter is not angry.
> A good winner is not vengeful,
> A good employer is humble.[21]

> A brave and passionate man will kill or be killed.
> A brave and calm man will always preserve life.[22]

From the Taoist perspective, the true enemies are not outside oneself. They are the demons of fear, anger, and hatred one harbors within.

To defeat this inner enemy, a person must awaken what in Chinese philosophy is called *chi*. Chi refers to a person's inner strength, a force that is distinctly different from one's outer physical strength. Physical strength fades with age, but the chi can actually become stronger as one matures, enabling a person to endure the trials of life and acquire great social influence that can last well beyond death.

The word chi, like the words *pneuma* in Greek and *ruach* in Hebrew, refers to both spirit and breath. This dual meaning implies life-energy, the influence of which is in direct proportion to one's virtue. It is virtue that strengthens chi. Conversely, the loss of virtue weakens the influence and respect a person wields. A strong chi also gives rise to foresight, a determined will, a focused energy, and clarity of mind. This clarity is maintained to the degree one is able to set aside anger, fear, vengeance, and selfish desire. In doing so, a person remains free from negative aggressive energy and thus can perceive clearly the path to balance and reconciliation. Again, to quote the Tao Te Ching,

> In caring for others and serving heaven,
> There is nothing like using restraint.
> Restraint begins with giving up one's own ideas.
> This depends on virtue gathered in the past.
> If there is a good store of virtue, then nothing is impossible.[23]

Through the foresight provided by the development of Chi, one can cultivate the awareness needed to avert the dangers that may potentially lie ahead.

> Peace is easily maintained;
> Trouble is easily overcome before it starts . . .
> Deal with it before it happens.
> Set things in order before there is confusion.[24]

Father-Son Reconciliation

In the fall of 1988, I had the opportunity to talk at some length over lunch and dinner with American poet Robert Bly. Along with his fame as a poet, Bly has become known for holding highly successful men's conferences. One purpose of these conferences is to teach men how to express their innate aggressive energy in constructive ways. Another purpose is to help them overcome the fear of their more sensitive, feminine side. According to Bly, both men and women have had to deal with shame, and they are afraid of being shamed. Women are much better at expressing their feelings, while men are reluctant to be open and tend to repress their shame. Bly believes a man has to be socialized into being a nurturing father. For reasons rooted in evolution and survival, nurturing behavior, he points out, is not common among male primates. It is much easier to train a man to be a warrior than to socialize him into being a nurturing father.[25]

Bly further asserts that men must learn to become sensitive and expressive, to rechannel and vent their anger and aggression in ways that do not cause harm. He is also an advocate of mentoring; men of maturity must help guide young boys into adulthood. Today, such mentors for young people are often provided in the arts and through participation in athletics. The ancient Taoist system of education appealed to a young man's warrior instinct by teaching him a martial art. At the same time, it developed his more sensitive, expressive nature by exposing him to the feminine, maternal philosophy in the Tao Te Ching. The Taoist masters served as mentors who could guide the instruction of students in the ways of virtue, philosophy, self-confidence, restraint, and artistic expression.

Given that the warrior image is socially and biologically imprinted onto a man's self-image, a recent movement known as the Mankind Project has begun to redefine male warrior identity, creating a new masculine paradigm. The old male warrior model is based on stereotypical masculine expectations, which include the ability to dominate, control, survive in isolation, suppress feelings and lead by aggression. The twenty-first-century *New Warrior*, as defined by the Mankind Project, finds power in developing positive and loving attitudes, being connected to self and others while allowing himself to be vulnerable and accountable for his actions. The New Warrior seeks to strip away the façade of contrived self-image by coming to know himself to be an authentic and genuine human being. He spends time in devotion and service to family and community in addition to himself. According to its mission statement, the Mankind Project "promises to enable men to live lives of integrity, accountability, and connection to feeling." The statement continues by calling on men "to be of service to the community at large as individual men with a renewed sense of passion and responsibility and as communities of men working together to build relationships."[26]

Robert Bly's men's conferences also sought to close the relational distance between father and son. This relational distance is not only rooted in the father's patriarchal role as disciplinarian. It also arises from the perception that a father's love, in contrast to a mother's abiding love, is expressed conditionally based on achievement. In an effort to initiate reconciliation, a father attending one of Bly's conferences could bring his son at no extra cost. The son could then be present to hear his father express how significant and meaningful the experience of fatherhood has been in his life. Reconciliation between father and son is important both for psychological well-being and to bring closure and completeness to the father-son relationship.

An Answer without Words

My dad and I were fortunate to have reconciled our differences during his later years in life. I was present to see his body and outer strength fade, the acceptance of which was difficult for my once-athletic father. Our reconciliation occurred in life, particularly during his struggle with bone cancer, but the process was ultimately fulfilled in death. After his passing, I could at last feel completely united with him. It was as if his physical body was the obstacle, his outer strength getting in the way of our full embrace. Now that his body was gone, there was no barrier between us.

As my mother, brother, and I planned his funeral, I silently asked to know if my dad was indeed at peace. Initially I resolved that this question could never be answered until, on my return flight home, I gazed out the window of the plane and, to my astonishment, saw on the clouds below a rare event. It was a rainbow in the form of a complete and perfect circle.

A month later, my father appeared to me in a dream, and I knew then that his chi, his inner strength, did not die. My dad had awakened me at last, only this time it wasn't for school.

Peace, in the sense of the absence of war, is of little value to someone who is dying of hunger or cold. It will not remove the pain of torture inflicted on a prisoner of conscience. It does not comfort those who have lost their loved ones in floods caused by senseless deforestation in a neighboring country. Peace can only last where human rights are respected, where the people are fed, and where individuals and nations are free.

—His Holiness, the Dalai Lama

Chapter 6

Violence and Religious Mythology

Though force can protect in emergency, only justice, fairness, consideration and co-operation can finally lead men to the dawn of eternal peace.

—Dwight D. Eisenhower

Theologian Walter Wink calls it the Myth of Redemptive Violence. It is one of the most thought-provoking ideas introduced into the field of peace studies over the past decade. Professor Wink derives his concept of redemptive violence from the Enuma Elish, an ancient Babylonian creation myth that dates from about 1250 BCE. In this story, creation is the result of a gruesome act of violence. Marduk, a god who is the superhero in the myth, murders and dismembers Tiamat, the mother god and dragon of chaos. He slits open her skull, scatters her blood, and from her corpse creates the cosmos. To quote Professor Wink in his book *The Powers That Be,*

> In this myth, creation is an act of violence. Marduk murders and dismembers Tiamat, and from her cadaver creates the world. As the French philosopher Paul Ricoeur observes [in *The Symbolism of Evil,* Harper Collins, 1967], order is established by means of disorder. Chaos (symbolized by Tiamat) is prior to order

(represented by Marduk, high god of Babylon). Evil precedes good. The gods themselves are violent.[1, *]

Figure 6
Marduk slays Tiamat, the dragon of chaos
Creation as resulting from an act of violence

---

*   In the most ancient Hindu scripture, the Rig-Veda, there is also a creation myth of dismemberment, although not so overtly violent as in the Babylonian story. Hymn 90 of the tenth mandala of the Rig-Veda depicts Purusha, the unified cosmic spirit, as a giant primeval man. He is the ruler of immortality who is bound for the primordial sacrifice and then dismembered by the gods to bring forth creation (O'Flaherty, *Rig Veda*, 30-31). Another rendition is found in Essene and Gnostic theology where there is said to have existed a spiritual body of light referred to as the primordial Adam. In the Gnostic myth, the primordial body of light is broken up into pieces of light, each piece becoming a soul to be born into the world. In the Gospel of John, this Gnostic image is recast in the parable of the sheepfold where the sheep, representing the souls of light, are scattered by the wolf, the wolf symbolizing the forces of darkness. Within these myths, however, there is also the promise that unity will one day be restored by a redeemer who comes to rejoin the souls of light into the great spiritual body (see John 10: 14-16; also see Davies, *The First Christian*, 120-121).

The Myth of Redemptive Violence is an archetypal story where a superhero, representing Good, is pitted against an equally powerful villain, representing Evil. After much struggle and suffering, the superhero uses violence to finally vanquish the villain, restoring order and reestablishing Good over Evil. One sees this archetypal plot reenacted time and again in movies such as *Batman*, *Superman*, and *Star Wars* and in cartoons like *Popeye the Sailor Man*, *Teenage Mutant Ninja Turtles*, and *Spiderman*.[2]

According to Wink, the Myth of Redemptive Violence

> Enshrines the belief that violence saves, that war brings peace, that might makes right. It is one of the oldest continuously repeated stories in the world.[3]

> The Myth of Redemptive Violence is the story of the victory of order over chaos by means of violence. It is the ideology of conquest, the original religion of the status quo.[4]

Professor Wink also argues that the biblical creation myth found in the first chapter of Genesis exists in stark contrast to the Babylonian story.*

> The biblical myth in Genesis 1 is diametrically opposed to all this [Genesis 1, it should be noted, was developed in Babylon during the Jewish captivity there as a direct rebuttal to the Babylonian myth]. The Bible portrays a good God who creates a good creation. Chaos does not resist order. Good is prior to evil. Neither evil nor violence is part of the creation, but enter later, as a result of the first couple's sin and the connivance of the serpent (Genesis 3). A basically good reality is thus corrupted by free decisions reached by creatures. In this far more complex and subtle explanation of the origins of things, violence emerges for the first time as a problem requiring solution.[5]

---

* There are actually two creation stories in Genesis, the second of which is in chapter 2. In chapter 1, Adam, the prototypical man, is created last. In chapter 2, he is created first. It is believed the story told in Genesis 2 was written earlier. Both these biblical creation myths are nonviolent. It is in chapter 4, when Adam's son Cain kills his brother Abel, that violence becomes part of the human experience.

In reflecting on the differences in these creation stories, I began to look for other nonviolent creation myths that are harmonious and transformational rather than violent. The ancient Lenape Native American story, for example, depicts the earth being raised out of the primordial waters on the back of a turtle. There is no violence present in the Lenape myth. As I explained in chapter 5, creation images found in the Tao Te Ching portray the creative force as female, the "mother" of heaven and earth. She is not evil chaos but a great mystery that gives birth to multiplicity as expressed in the phrase, "ten thousand things."*

Despite these nonviolent, transformational creation myths, violent biblical creation stories have had a far more enduring influence on the human psyche. Later in Genesis, for example, after seeing that the ways of humans are evil, God destroys the world with a violent all-consuming flood. And centuries later, the Day of Judgment is described in the book of Revelation as a violent event with the great final battle of Armageddon preceding the triumphant return of Christ.

Merging Myth with History

Violent myths were most often told by people who emerged victorious from war. Later, their stories became part of religiously inspired histories. Jewish writers were exceptionally good at integrating myth and history and did so in such a convincing manner that, for many people, it is difficult to determine where history leaves off and myth begins.

For example, the history of the Israelites, as told in the book of Exodus, begins with the Israelites as slaves in Egypt. Upon their escape, they migrate from Egypt through the desert, eventually settling in the land of Canaan, which they believe to be their Promised Land. But included in this history is the story of God having Moses stretch out his arms to part the Red Sea. The Israelites pass through on dry land, after which the waters return to destroy the pursuing Egyptian army.[6] Myth or history? Allegorically, the separation of the waters can be viewed as a birth metaphor intended to symbolize the birthing of a new nation.† It also teaches that when we confront an insurmountable obstacle, if our intentions are pure, a force far greater than ourselves will allow us to pass through.

---

*   Tao Te Ching, chapter 25. In some translations, "ten thousand things" is translated as "myriad things."

†   Before a woman gives birth, her water breaks, signaling the beginning of labor.

Figure 7
The Red Sea engulfs the Egyptian army
From *Figures de la Bible* (1728) attributed by Gerard Hoet (1648-1733)
In religiously inspired histories, one man's miracle can be another
man's tragedy.

Earlier in Exodus, when Moses questions whether his people would believe him, God commands him to cast the rod he was carrying onto the ground, whereupon it turns into a serpent, only to become a rod again when Moses picks it up.[7] An allegorical interpretation suggests this mythological embellishment testifies to the conquering power of God's wisdom over evil, the serpent intended as a symbol for temptation and deception as it was so used in the Garden of Eden myth.*

---

*   As an allegory, the story of the Exodus provided inspiration for African slaves in the United States, images of which are expressed often in Negro spirituals. The Southern slaveholder became the pharaoh; freedom in the north, the Promised Land; and Harriet Tubman, who covertly led many slaves to freedom using the safe houses of the Underground Railroad, became known as the black Moses.

Mystics view the story of the Exodus as an allegorical journey to spiritual enlightenment. The slavery of the Israelites is a metaphor for being in bondage to

The miracle of the Jewish Passover, in which God sends a plague killing the firstborn male in every Egyptian household in a final attempt to convince Pharaoh to free the Israelites from slavery, presents us with a more perplexing dilemma. Consider the Passover story from the vantage point of a young Egyptian wife. After three years of marriage, she finally gives birth to a son who subsequently dies from the plague. When told it was the god of the Israelites who sent this plague to free his people from Pharaoh's bondage, she sees nothing but injustice. She, her husband, and her son had nothing to do with enslaving the Jews. It was Pharaoh who was responsible. Why would God commit such a horrible genocidal act, the killing of innocent children, to liberate a people? In this religiously inspired history, one man's miracle turns out to be another man's tragedy.

It can be argued that, in the ancient world, such violent creation and recreation myths played a much-needed socio-evolutionary role in holding together disparate tribes and building a sense of nationhood. In our modern world, however, they too often reinforce divisive religious beliefs that convince people that violence is an inevitable part of the human condition, even a holy response. Unless we can separate myth from history, we run the risk of deluding ourselves into believing that acts of violence are foreordained, or that God is on our side.

Unintended Consequences

Iraq was a country President George W. Bush included in his three-nation "axis of evil," the remaining two being Iran and North Korea. The buildup to the 2003 United States invasion of Iraq illustrates how political leaders tend to make unrealistic projections when it comes to waging war.

Before the war began on March 20 of 2003, U.S. secretary of defense Donald Rumsfeld predicted Iraqi oil revenues of between $18 and $20 billion would offset the cost of the war and Iraqi reconstruction. A few months later, President Bush asked the U.S. Congress for $87 billion to

---

ignorance. To be lost in the wilderness symbolizes the personal quest to free oneself from repetitive negative habits (i.e., a person who is lost tends to walk in circles or make the same mistakes in life over and over). Entering the Promised Land represents the liberation of the spirit which is the culmination of the path to enlightenment.

finance military operations.[8] After seven years of engagement, the cost had ballooned to $700 billion. Secretary Rumsfeld insisted that U.S. Intelligence knew the general location of weapons of mass destruction in and around Tikrit and Baghdad, yet none were ever found.[9] And roughly three months after the beginning of the war, President George W. Bush made his infamous speech aboard the aircraft carrier USS *Abraham Lincoln* declaring "mission accomplished." The war continued, however, for at least another seven years, becoming what Rumsfeld called "a long, hard slog." U.S. soldiers killed in Iraq exceeded 4,000, more than the number of civilians killed on 9/11, and well over 30,000 U.S. soldiers were seriously wounded. Whether out of ignorance or out of the obsession for political power, U.S. political leaders clearly misjudged the enemy insurgency and had little awareness of the "law of unintended consequences," a force that is always unleashed along with dogs of war.

Undoubtedly, one of the unintended consequences of the U.S. invasion of Iraq has been the accelerated nuclear ambition of Iran and North Korea. The United States launched the second Iraq war believing Iraqi president Saddam Hussein possessed biological weapons of mass destruction. This belief turned out to be wrong. Would the United States have invaded Iraq had Saddam Hussein possessed nuclear weapons? Iranian and North Korean leaders believe the answer is no. Although Iran and North Korea have long had an interest in nuclear technology, America's invasion of Iraq in 2003 motivated both nations to accelerate development of nuclear weapons as a deterrent should the United States or Israel choose the preemptive option.*

One can view peace studies as the investigation of how to minimize the influence of the law of unintended consequences. Compare, for example, four formal methods for dealing with conflict, these being (1) mediation, (2) arbitration, (3) litigation, and (4) physical violence, which, of course, includes war. During mediation, all that is aired remains confidential. A facilitator sits with the parties in conflict and helps them articulate their differences so they clearly understand each other's respective complaints. An effort is then made to find common ground on which to forge an agreement both parties can accept.

When utilizing the second strategy, the conflicting parties go before an arbitrator who has the authority to impose a solution. While the solution is

---

*   North Korea detonated its first nuclear device on October 9, 2006.

not legally binding, the parties are usually in a subordinate position to the arbitrator who is often a boss or superior administrator.

Litigation involves settling the dispute through the legal system. Attorneys are hired or assigned to represent the persons in conflict, and a judge then imposes a ruling that can be legally enforced.

The fourth strategy, physical violence or war, abandons all forms of negotiation and strives to force a solution on one's adversary.

During mediation, the parties in conflict have full control over the outcomes as mediation allows both parties to accept only what they can agree to. The risk for unintended consequences surfacing is very low. As one proceeds through the methods of arbitration and litigation, the risk of unintended consequences increases since an arbitrator or judge may impose a solution and not require agreement by the involved parties. The outcomes from violent confrontations are the most unpredictable, with war in particular being especially sloppy and disastrous. While generals and politicians often speak as if the outcomes of military operations are surgical and under their control, history teaches otherwise. The law of unintended consequences is given free rein when we choose the path of violence.

Redemptive Violence and Classical Military Strategies

Outside the domain of myth, redemptive violence can be defined as hostile acts committed out of the belief that individuals can redeem themselves through violence, or that violence will liberate a person from an earthly struggle leading to a heavenly reward. It is an ideology that has fueled many a religious war and invites volunteer martyrdom like we see in modern-day terrorism. Classical military strategies are generally ineffective against redemptive violence for the following reasons:

1. Military campaigns are oriented toward achieving a victorious end to the conflict while combatants engaged in redemptive violence are in a position where they do not have to win—all they have to do is continue their struggle and not lose.

2. Classical military efforts are usually motivated by the defense of interests while redemptive violence is fed by poverty, desperation, and the deluded notion of rewards in an afterlife.

3. Military strategists think geographically, seeking to seize or protect a defined territory while those engaged in redemptive violence think non-geographically—they are not bound by borders.

4. Under a classical military system, soldiers are recruited or drafted and fight out of duty, personal honor, or for what is viewed as a worthy social or political cause. In contrast, combatants engaged in redemptive violence undergo conversion to an ideology and form an insurgency to fight out of religious conviction.
5. In classical military systems, there is a top-down chain of command where soldiers answer to their superior while those engaged in redemptive violence adopt more of a networking style of organization, functioning as autonomous or semi-autonomous "cells."

Ironically, using military force against religiously motivated violence is often counterproductive in that it plays into the hands of the perpetrators, providing them the opportunity to fulfill their redemptive mission. It also tends to strengthen rather than weaken the enemy as siblings and relatives seek vengeance for the death of their family members. The result is often a condition of low-grade perpetual war as we have seen in the ongoing conflicts in the Middle East.

The Bush administration's war on terror, initiated shortly after 9/11, was unfortunately a World War II solution to a twenty-first-century problem. Publicly declaring it a war merely elevated the status of Osama bin Laden on the international stage, making it easier for him and Al-Qaeda to attract new recruits. Bin Laden and his followers did not deserve such recognition and, instead, should have been dealt with solely as international criminals.

What the Bush administration failed to realize is that Osama bin Laden was not seeking a military victory over the United States. His aim was to bring the United States down economically, and the global recession that began in 2008 nearly fulfilled his goal. For him, the World Trade Center was America's Tower of Babel, a symbol of Western secularism and its insatiable thirst for economic power and materialism. Homegrown insurgencies—as we have seen emerge in the seemingly unending conflicts in the Middle East, Iraq, and Afghanistan—are succeeding in making war increasingly costly, unwinnable, and perhaps even obsolete. The realization of the limits of military force, however, creates the recognition that the military should play a peace-building as well as a policing and peacekeeping role. In conjunction with nongovernmental organizations, it must also restore community infrastructure, build schools, provide medical clinics and financial assistance to win the hearts and minds of the people and convince them to resist the destructive insurgency. Such a road is long and expensive, but it is a significant step forward in the way politicians view the use of a military presence.

Peace-Building in Israel and Afghanistan

Regardless of the form of government, be it democratic, theocratic, authoritarian, or a monarchy, political posturing by national leaders and the quest to stay in power creates one of the biggest obstacles to peace-building. When their country is threatened or attacked, there is the tendency for politicians to talk tough, over-react, or respond disproportionately. The maxim "An eye for an eye and a tooth for a tooth" was originally intended to temper revenge so that injustice can be responded to in a way that is proportional to the initial hostile infraction. Unfortunately, an act of retaliation tends to exceed the damage caused by the original aggressor, resulting in escalation, rather than a cessation, of the conflict. Hence came Gandhi's famous retort: "An eye for an eye makes the whole world blind."

A typical example is the Israeli invasion of Gaza in the fall of 2008. Conducted to stop Palestinian militants from hurling harassing unguided rockets into Israel, the military incursion by the Israelis swept through neighborhoods in Gaza and killed over 700 Palestinian civilians. On the Israeli side, less than ten civilians died. While in the short-term such incursions may succeed in reducing life-threatening harassment, in the long-term they deepen generational hatred and strengthen support for advocates of violence. In the case of Israel, such heavy-handed disproportionate military campaigns distract from the long history of Palestinian suicide bombings and, in the eyes of public opinion, make the Israelis look like the aggressors.

Political pressures make it difficult for leaders to seek reconciliation for fear they may appear weak, and the escalation of violence merely adds to the history of hostility that widens the gulf between nations or peoples in conflict. For these reasons, peace-building efforts generally have more lasting success when they originate on the grassroots level. Over time, grassroots movements change the political landscape. New generations step into leadership roles with a less tarnished view of history, and politicians emerge that are able to entertain reforms. One can see how this played out in the United States as the civil rights movement changed attitudes in America toward racism and segregation. In the Soviet Union, it was the younger generation that produced a leader like Mikhail Gorbachev who brought a new vision to Russia in the late 1980s. With the emergence of the Green Movement in Iran, it is likely we will see the liberalization of Iranian politics if the West allows time for younger leaders to enter into positions of influence. As Senator John McCain has astutely observed, "The birth of the Green Movement over the past year should convince us that Iran will have a democratic future. That future may be delayed for a while, but it will not be denied."[10]

In Israel, there are significant efforts that exemplify grassroots peace-building and which show long-term promise. One is the Nazareth Academic Institute (NAI) located in Nazareth, Galilee, in Israel. Affiliated with Mar Elias College, the program brings together Israeli and Palestinian students from diverse religious backgrounds.* In addition, several Arab-Jewish bilingual elementary schools have been established in Israel with each classroom presided over by an Arab and an Israeli teacher. One of their central objectives is to teach an accurate view of Israeli and Palestinian history.†

Afghanistan has also been a stage for grassroots peace-building through education. There is a dynamic multifaith organization where I live that is led by two prominent Muslims who immigrated to the United States from Afghanistan. This philanthropic organization, called *Awaken*, has built a school to educate girls and a women's medical clinic. The facilities they have provided are now rendering services in a remote Afghan village. The week after 9/11, my Muslim friends who founded *Awaken* received threatening telephone calls. They could not believe such harassment could happen in America. This is what they came to America to escape!

On a much larger scale, an organization known as the Central Asia Institute has built well over one hundred schools in remote regions in Pakistan and Afghanistan with one of its goals also being to educate young girls. In 1993, mountain climber Greg Mortenson failed in his attempt to scale K2, the world's second-highest peak. In the book *Three Cups of Tea: One Man's Mission to Promote Peace . . . One School at a Time*, Mortensen tells the story of his rescue by villagers and the life-changing experience that led to his promise to build a school for their children.[11] The result has been a remarkable peace-building effort with Taliban tribal warlords that has been recognized by government officials in Pakistan and the United States.

As the present U.S. military and political quagmire in Afghanistan grows old, we will finally rid ourselves of our terrorist paranoia. While we must keep a watchful eye on terrorism through policing and intelligence gathering, we must also seek to build cooperative relationships with Islamic cultures, providing medical, educational, and employment opportunities

---

*   For more information on the Nazareth Academic Institute, go to www.mecedu.org.

†   For more on Israeli/Palestinian schools, see www.youtube.com/watch?v=DaSL_S3_xhg, and www.youtube.com/watch?v=SKo4-Hu0BdQ&feature=related.

as our means of overcoming hatred. Military solutions leave in their wake repressed hostilities; strategies of reconciliation entice people to embrace positive alternatives to violence. To paraphrase Martin Luther King Jr., we must counter their force with soul force, and we must match their ability to hate with our ability to love.[12]

Change, Globalization, and Cultural Dissonance

Must new creations necessarily arise out of violence? Or, in terms of social and political reform, is violence really necessary to change or transform a society?

If we look to the natural world, we do certainly see creation arising out of violence. It was a violent volcanic eruption that created the awesome and picturesque coastline on the Caribbean island of St. Lucia. The Earth's violent collision with an asteroid is now believed to have led to the demise of the dinosaurs, making possible the evolution and ascent of human life on earth. Even the beginning of the universe is now said to have resulted from a primordial explosion, the "big bang" as it is called.

Yet the natural world also reveals harmonious creative processes of rebirth and transformation that are not violent and disruptive. In the earth's temperate zones, such a process can be observed every spring as life reawakens from lying dormant during the winter months. Indeed, the earth's landscape is continuously being reformed and reshaped by natural forces. Rivers slowly modify their courses, carving out deep canyons as the wind, over time, erodes mountain peaks, and plant succession creates old-growth forests.

These natural, harmonious transformations are gradual and not cataclysmic. They occur slowly enough so that species, living in their natural habitats, are able to adapt to the changing environment rather than face the threat of extinction. The lesson that can be taken from this is that while social, economic, and environmental change is inevitable, governments should strive to manage the pace of change so their citizens can meet the challenge of adapting to a shifting economy with minimal hardship. Unfortunately, human beings tend to be impatient, provoking change in ways that is too often detrimental to our planet and the human condition. A relevant example is the push toward capitalist globalization at the beginning of this century that proceeded too rapidly without proper economic regulation.

Multinational corporations can have a positive impact on developing countries. They frequently offer training and education for the skilled labor required for their workforce, provide employment opportunities for women and, over the long-term, raise the standard of living in poor countries. Furthermore, as women become more active in the workforce, the birth rate tends to be lower, thus helping to curb population growth.

However, large businesses also can have a serious negative impact. There is a tendency for multinational corporations to buy up large tracts of land that had been used to support a diversified agriculture which supplied a variety of crops to the local population. Agricultural corporations then focus on raising one or two large crops, and manufacturers use land for building production facilities, thereby reducing the indigenous crop diversity in the local food supply. They also tend to disrupt local economies by paying higher wages to local workers that are disproportionate to the local economic norm. Resentment is created between local residents hired by the corporations and those who are not chosen for work. Such economic disruption causes inflation in land values and in the price of locally produced goods. The country's poor adult population then has more difficulty providing for their families.

In addition, many developing countries do not have laws to prevent the exploitation of labor and protect against child labor. The results are extended-hour workweeks with no overtime pay, poor working conditions, sweatshops, and parents choosing to have their children forego education to work in the factories or fields because they need the money to support the family.*

Globalization has made it easier for multinational corporations to operate in countries where protective labor laws do not exist. In addition, American domestic workers suffer the consequences of outsourcing and the loss of secure jobs as production facilities are moved overseas. If the United States is to contribute successfully to the growth and management of a global economy, it must lead by example, pressing for labor laws comparable to those in the United States and adopting a code of ethics that protects workers in countries where the exploitation of labor is common. It must also keep its own financial house in order to prevent another global economic recession like the one in 2008, which threatened the economies of the major industrialized nations. The danger of such mismanagement is

---

*   For a moving personal account of how the rapid infusion of Western industrialization disrupts village economies, see *Nectar in a Sieve* by Kamala Markandaya, New York: Signet Books, pages 29-34.

growing regional conflicts as economies falter, the environment deteriorates, and countries are forced into competing for increasingly scarce resources.

The infusion of Western multinational corporations into Eastern and Middle Eastern countries also has had a disrupting cultural impact. Sometimes referred to as cultural imperialism (I prefer to call it cultural dissonance), it is most blatantly expressed through the generally unrestricted Internet, the clash of religious conservatism with liberal religious theology, and the rejection by Islamic nations of feminism, permissiveness, and the pursuit of happiness through material excess.

In the 1980s, Iranian religious leader Ayatollah Khomeini called the United States "the Great Satan," a label meant to condemn Western secular values. Americans, however, generally misunderstand this expression. In mystical religious traditions, Satan signifies that force in human life that draws the senses outward into the physical world and away from the inner spiritual life. This distraction deceives one into believing that lasting happiness can be found in materialism and the gratification of sexual desires. From the perspective of fundamentalist Muslims, as well as conservative Christians, Americans and Europeans have been guilty of cultivating a materialistic, sex-crazed culture.

Offensive cultural dissonance could be minimized if Western nations and multinational corporations would be more sensitive to the cultural values of nations they are interfacing with, especially through the Internet. As Westerners, we fail to realize how some countries see the Internet, with its worldwide accessibility, as an instrument of cultural imperialism. Multinational corporations should, preferably on a voluntary basis, be more responsible when evaluating, for example, sexually provocative messages conveyed in images used in commercial advertising and on Internet websites. While some might view this as an intrusion on free speech, such compromises would be well worth it given the great advantages of cultural interfacing, which include the gradual improvement of human rights, educational and economic cooperation, interfaith cultural understanding, and the emerging professional role of women in developing countries.

Narcissistic Injury

Sigmund Freud and other psychological theorists have argued that social pressures force us to repress our aggressive urges.[13] Over time, this repression creates inner conflict until our aggressive tendencies are given an opportunity to be expressed in the "legalized" violence of war. These urges are then cut loose, and a person is able to fulfill their aggressive subconscious desires through war. If Freud is correct, humans will always need police and government military organizations to provide retaliatory capabilities as a deterrent to the expression of their repressed aggressive behavior.

A counterargument to Freud's explanation is that deterrence to aggression also can be provided through positive means. That is, rather than deterring violence with the threat of negative consequences, such as fines, imprisonment, or violent retaliation, the deterrence can be a symbiotic relationship, the benefits of which would be lost if the rules that sustain the cooperative relationship are violated. The more a society makes use of positive methods of deterrence, the less reliance there would be on police, jails, and the military.

Freud also proposed that injury and rage have their psychological roots in narcissism.[14] In Greek and Roman mythologies, Narcissus was a handsome young hunter who fell in love with his own image as reflected in a pool of water. He thus is a metaphor for excessive self-love and self-identification. Narcissistic injury occurs when you take as a personal attack an injury to a member of the group to which you belong or self-identify. One perceives that their expanded or inflated sense of self is being attacked, either verbally or physically.

If someone attacks a member of your family and you react as if it were an attack on either your own life or your personal self-identity, you are experiencing narcissistic injury; if, in your anger, you decide in return to attack a member of your aggressor's family (other than the person who was actually responsible for the original attack), you are engaging in a calculated form of "narcissistic rage" or what may be called narcissistic revenge. The group to which you belong, however, can be much larger than your family. It can be defined by the race to which you belong, your nationality, or your religious sect.

Surprisingly, such vengeful behavior is not unique to humans. Michael McCullough, a professor at the University of Miami in Coral Gables, was astonished to find that Japanese macaques, if harmed by a high-ranking individual in their community, would retaliate by abusing a low-ranking relative of the monkey that inflicted the harm.[15]

In November of 2004, I received a phone call from a Chicago resident concerned about what I taught in my peace studies class on nonviolence. During the course of the conversation, the caller, when referring to the 9/11 terrorist plot, exclaimed, "We were attacked!" Such a reaction is an example of narcissistic injury. The caller was not in New York or Washington DC on 9/11. He was not *personally* attacked physically, but nevertheless, saw himself as threatened because he was identifying with the Americans who were in the World Trade Center or the Pentagon.

Immediately after 9/11, there were some instances where U.S. citizens sought revenge against Muslims living in the United States solely because the 9/11 hijackers were Muslim. Not only were these Americans experiencing narcissistic injury, they were engaging in narcissistic revenge.*

Once a conflict is elevated to this level of psychological intensity, the number of people that join the conflict can increase exponentially because revenge is being taken against individuals who were not initially part of the dispute. People involved in the conflict no longer are seeking justice against the actual perpetrators but are pursuing revenge against a group that has been stereotyped. In seeking such narcissistic revenge, the conflicting parties broaden the scope of the conflict, drawing into the fray relatives, friends, and associates who then experience feelings of narcissistic injury that motivate future attacks. We thus have a psychological model that explains why insurgencies, such as those encountered in wars in Iraq and Afghanistan, battle defiantly to sustain themselves and at times appear to grow stronger. What is in play here is a kind of group neurosis that is fed by violence and is virtually impossible to defeat militarily.

Because of these psychological underpinnings, we have little reason to be optimistic that humanity will ever overcome its predilection for violence, especially when fueled by religious fervor. Mahatma Gandhi was forced to confront this reality in 1946. After all his teaching and past nonviolent campaigns that united people of diverse faiths, Hindus and Muslims were at each other's throats, going on murderous rampages though villages and city neighborhoods. It was a time of great cynicism for the Mahatma. For a moment, he even reflected on his life as a failure.[16] But it was not Gandhi who had failed.

Throughout history, power and revenge have proven themselves at times to consume the masses. Resorting to violence is often a temptation politicians, and the people who follow them, find hard to resist. In 2003, between 75 and 80 percent of Americans supported the invasion of Iraq[17]

---

*   In one instance, a Sikh named Balbir Singh Sodhi, who was wearing his turban but was mistaken for a Muslim, was gunned down on September 15, 2001, in Mesa, Arizona. Before the murder, his killer bragged of his intention to "kill the ragheads responsible for September 11" (www. themediaoasis.com/hatevictims.html).

despite the fact that weapons of mass destruction had not been found, and none of the 9/11 hijackers were Iraqis. The United States, which had prided itself in being a nation that only would use weapons to defend itself and its allies against armed aggression, was now engaging in preemptive war.

We therefore must not be naïve about the public's political perception of war, especially when military might is available, because for the victor, violence *does* save. But what it saves is the material rather than the spiritual; what it saves are the treasures we have laid up on earth, not the treasures we are to lay up in heaven.[18] What it saves are worldly interests and attachments at the expense of a nation losing its soul.

Embracing Uncertainty

In May of 2007, I was invited to the Caribbean nation of St. Lucia to give three workshops on nonviolence and conflict resolution. The workshops were offered to school administrators at the request of the minister of education, who was extremely supportive and enthusiastic about the emerging field of peace studies. After my third lecture, I was taken to a restaurant that had a sheltered patio. There we sat beneath a canopy as we waited to savor some delectable Caribbean cuisine. Suddenly, on the stone patio wall a safe distance from where we were sitting, we saw a large centipede. I was intrigued by its reddish color as it slowly crept along the wall. The minister of education, however, did not share my fascination. She started screaming, removed one of her shoes, aggressively walked over to the wall, and proceeded to beat the centipede to death with the heel of her shoe.

After the "threat" was removed, I reminded her that she invited me to lecture on nonviolence and asked her why she killed the insect. It suddenly dawned on her how contradictory her behavior was. This centipede was not close to us and was clearly no danger to anyone in the restaurant. Her action was based solely on an inner fear and on what she perceived as "ugly." This incident reveals that, regardless of how much people talk about peace and nonviolence, there are reactions rooted in fear that erupt almost as an involuntary response.

Teaching compassion and nonviolence requires that we instill in each person both the wisdom and the ability to restrain and subdue such irrational reactions. We must conquer our primitive defense mechanisms that respond out of fear and deceive the mind into believing that violence is the answer. For ultimately, the Myth of Redemptive Violence takes place within us. It is an allegory for the human condition.

Subconsciously, each one of us wishes we could emerge as Marduk, the superhero who destroys Tiamat, the dragon of chaos. But the dragon is little more than a centipede, and the enemy we must slay is actually within us. We seek to end the uncertainty we fear as chaos by imposing, through whatever means necessary, our own vision of order and justice. By recognizing and renouncing this gripping primal urge, we learn to embrace uncertainty rather than resist it. A higher path is then revealed, one that recognizes the enemy's gifts and uses conflict to our advantage. The negative power conflict has over us is converted into a positive regenerative force which, as we shall see in chapter 7, is capable of transforming death into life.

Time itself becomes subordinate to war. If only we could celebrate peace as our various ancestors celebrated war; if only we could glorify peace as those before us, thirsting for adventure, glorified war; if only our sages and scholars together could resolve to infuse peace with the same energy and inspiration that others have put into war.

—Elie Wiesel

Chapter 7

Earth Day, Easter, and the Current Mass Extinction

Mother Earth hears the call; she awakens, she arises; she feels the breath of the new born Dawn. The leaves and the grass stir; all things move with the breath of the new day. Everywhere life is renewed . . . we are speaking of something very sacred, although it happens every day.

—The Kurahus, Hako,
Birth of Dawn, Pawnee

Mahatma Gandhi said, "The world has enough for everyone's need, but not enough for everyone's greed."[1] His words force us to ponder the difference between living with what we require for our reasonable comfort and what we long for out of wanton selfishness.

Two centuries ago, the thinking was quite different. It was believed that the world would eventually reach the point where it could *not* supply everyone's need. This conclusion was expressed in what became known as the Malthusian theory. English clergyman and mathematician Thomas Malthus asserted that humanity's exponential population growth would eventually outpace food production. His theory influenced Charles Darwin and served as the prevailing worldview from the nineteenth to the mid-twentieth century. In 1968, Paul R. Ehrlich published the controversial book *The Population Bomb*. Ehrlich envisioned what others called a Malthusian catastrophe with mass famine and starvation occurring in the 1970s and '80s, a prediction that fortunately did not materialize.

Prior to Ehrlich, there were many who questioned Malthus' conclusion. Wars, natural disasters and falling fertility rates due to industrialization were cited as mechanisms that would curb population growth.

In 1969, R. Buckminster Fuller, the visionary architect and designer of the geodesic dome, published his *Operating Manual for Spaceship Earth*. Like others before him, Fuller challenged the idea of a Malthusian catastrophe. His argument, however, was grounded not in the occurrence of wars and natural disasters but in the first law of thermodynamics, known as the law of conservation of energy. Fuller explained that while energy is finite, it is also "infinitely conserved."[2] Energy may be transferred from one state to another (e.g., from potential energy to kinetic energy), but we cannot exhaust the energy we have available to us. Moreover, the earth is an open system, sustained by virtually unlimited energy from the sun. Thus, humans potentially have all the energy required to provide for the earth's population. We simply need to harness the vast amount of energy available to us. In Fuller's words, the "main engine" of spaceship earth, "the life regenerating processes, must operate exclusively on our vast daily energy income from the powers of wind, tide, water, and the direct sun radiation energy."[3]

Fuller further recognized that complex systems behave in ways that cannot be predicted by the behavior of the system's complex individual parts. This concept is referred to as "synergy." Fuller observed synergy at work in the universe and in the evolution of life. He saw the universe as a "mammoth perpetual motion process"[4] that was "evolving without beginning or end."[5] Life, therefore, must be regenerative by nature, and it should be humanity's goal not to compete for resources but instead, work cooperatively to capitalize on our sun-earth system's synergy and regenerative power.

In asserting life's perpetually regenerative nature, Fuller was using twentieth-century scientific jargon to revisit an idea expressed thousands of years ago in ancient myth and religion. The Native American poet quoted at the beginning of this chapter expressed it less scientifically when he wrote, "All things move with the breath of the new day. Everywhere life is renewed . . . we are speaking of something very sacred, although it happens every day." To the tribal shamans, the sacred is all around us, expressing itself each day in the blooming of a flower, the birth of a child, the rising of the sun, the radiance of the moon, or the changing of the seasons. While indigenous Americans were forced to acclimate to the European invaders and eventually to the industrial age, their spiritual awareness has preserved a connection to, and an appreciation for, the regenerative power seen in the natural world.

America's greatest natural philosopher, Henry David Thoreau, in observing the breaking up of ice on Walden Pond during the early spring, expressed it more poetically:

> It is glorious to behold this ribbon of water sparkling in the sun, the bare face of the pond full of glee and youth, as if it spoke the joy of the fishes within it, and of the sands on its shore . . . Such a contrast between winter and spring. Walden was dead and is alive again.[6]

Surely it is fitting that the celebration of Earth Day falls so close to the vernal equinox and Easter as people celebrate the wondrous and sacred resurgence of life in the natural world each passing year.

The Triumphant Phoenix

The most prominent ancient myth to laud the regenerative power of creation was that of the phoenix. With wings of fire, this great mythological bird flies to earth from the sun to die by cremation. It then resurrects from its own ashes, concluding its life cycle by ascending back to heaven to reign supreme after its magnificent conquest of life's ultimate enemy, death.

Figure 8
The phoenix, also known as the sunbird or firebird

The oldest meaning attributed to this myth deals with the movement of the sun through the sky; the sun "dies" in the evening when it sets and is reborn each morning as it rises. In the ancient world, the myth also offered an explanation for how fire came to earth. Later, the phoenix came to reflect the ancient view that creation is self-sacrificial by design. As Alan Watts explains in his book *Myth and Ritual in Christianity*, "Every form of life exists at the expense of some other form."[7] Living things thrive by killing and devouring other forms of life. Life, in the generic sense, sacrifices itself to itself in order to perpetuate itself—every creature that is killed offering itself in sacrifice.

This great paradox, that life is actually sustained through death, was embodied in the phoenix myth, conveying the belief that death is not an end to life but rather, is a means through which it is transformed. In the science of thermodynamics, physical energy is subject to the first law of thermodynamics; i.e., energy is neither created nor destroyed but can change from one form to another. Analogously, in the ancient world, the life-energy that comprised the soul (*psyche* in Greek) was viewed as not being destroyed at the time of death but as taking on a different form.

It was believed that humans have a dual nature—a lower animal nature that is selfish, material, and temporal, and a higher spiritual nature which, while bound in the physical body, possesses moral integrity and is destined to ascend to its eternal heavenly home. We did not, however, have to wait until physical death to experience our higher spiritual nature. We simply had to undergo a trial in life, a period of adversity or "baptism by fire." This experience would awaken our higher spiritual nature, bestowing on us new life and the realization that the awareness, the spirit within, exists autonomously from the body. Such an experience would cause one to "die within" so that a person would be born a second time in this life.*

Anyone who appreciates natural philosophy will recognize the butterfly as a metaphor for this spiritual birth. The butterfly spends the first portion of its life groveling on the earth as a caterpillar, after which it enters its cocoon. Then, from a seemingly lifeless state, it emerges as a glorious creature, ascending to enjoy its newly acquired domain and power of flight. Thoreau, in his conclusion to *Walden*, uses a more earthy insect as a metaphor. He

---

* The apostle Paul writes of this mystical death when he metaphorically describes himself as having already been "crucified with Christ" (Galatians 2:20). Rumi, the Sufi poet, expresses it as follows: "Always see infinite life in letting the self die" (Mathnawi, vol. I, 1126-1127).

tells the story of a "strong and beautiful bug which came out of the dry leaf of an old table of apple-tree wood which had stood in a farmer's kitchen for 60 years . . . from an egg deposited in the living tree many years earlier . . . hatched perchance by the heat of an urn." He then asks: "Who does not feel his faith in resurrection and immortality strengthened by hearing of this?"[8] Long ago, someone must have pondered the question: are humans capable of such a metamorphosis, not physically, of course, but psychologically and spiritually?*

To fully appreciate this concept of second birth, we must understand that there are multiple ways to define life. The definition that initially comes to mind is what we learn in high school biology classes. The criteria for fulfilling this biological definition of life requires that an organism (1) exhibit metabolism, or the chemical transfer of energy within and among cells; (2) be able to reproduce; and (3) respond to stimuli. This classical biological definition is dualistic. Either the organism we are observing is alive or it is dead.

Nobel Prize-winning physicist Erwin Schrödinger developed an alternative definition of life, applying the concept of entropy from the field of thermodynamics. Entropy is the tendency in the universe for isolated systems to move from a condition of order to one of disorder or thermodynamic equilibrium. A rod of iron, for example, will eventually rust; a dead piece of wood will gradually decay. Schrödinger observed that a living system has the ability to evade or delay the inevitable trend toward entropy, or to extract "negative entropy" (i.e., order) from its environment.[9] His definition exposes the importance of preventing environmental degradation which is the breakdown of order in the natural world, and can be generalized to apply to the psychological domain. It suggests that to sustain life, cultivating intellectual, emotional, and aesthetic well-being is as important as maintaining physiological or biological order.†

---

*   In Christian scripture, the expression "born again" as translated from the Greek in the Gospel of John literally means "born from above." The concept of second birth also is found in Hinduism. The first birth refers to being born from the womb of one's mother; the second is a spiritual birth traditionally signified through an initiation by a spiritual teacher. The disciple is then said to be "twice born" (Nikhilananda, *The Upanishads*, vol. I, 4).

†   Despite the fact that life brings forth order from disorder, the overall effect, according to thermodynamics, is still an increase in entropy.

There is yet another view of life, however, that comprises an aesthetic or spiritual definition. Unlike the classical biological criteria, the aesthetic view of life is not dualistic. In this case, you can be more alive or less alive. The property of life can even be ascribed to something that is biologically lifeless. We say that a sculptor aesthetically infuses life into a piece of marble, or that the orchestra brought a Beethoven symphony to life. We may refer to someone as the "life of the party," or, if we are bored, speak of the party as "dead." And let's not forget the familiar phrase, "Life begins at forty!"

The Gospel of John quotes Jesus as saying, "I come that you may have life, and have it more abundantly."[10] In using such language, he clearly is not defining life in dualistic biological terms. It is the quality and meaning of life that is his standard. This most certainly includes the awakening we experience when we encounter a life-changing event. As Thoreau concisely expressed it in *Walden*, "To be awake is to be alive."[11] Second birth is a metaphor for this aesthetic and psychological awakening, whereby we perceive deeper meaning and find new direction in life. It is a spiritual metamorphosis that liberates us from the millstone of matter and the ignorance that propagates complacency and injustice.

While the story of the phoenix is most known as an Egyptian myth, it is perhaps the most pervasive myth of the ancient world. It is also found in Russian mythology where it is known as the firebird. Igor Stravinsky's "Firebird Suite" was composed to accompany the ballet version of this myth. The oldest written rendition of the phoenix is in the Hindu scripture known as the Rig Veda, where it is referred to as the sunbird. The following lines from the Rig Veda are devoted to this image. In these verses, *Varuna* refers to the "guardian of sacred laws and cosmic order," and the word *Yama* is the Hindu name for the god of death.

> Longing for you in their heart, they saw you flying to the dome
> of the sky as an eagle, the golden winged messenger of Varuna,
> the bird hastening into the womb of Yama.
>
> Then the divine youth climbed straight back up to the dome of
> the sky bearing his many-colored weapons.*

---

*   The sunbird's "many-colored weapons" were used not for war, but to conquer death and thereby vanquish what was perceived as life's ultimate enemy.

Dressing himself in a perfumed robe, looking like sunlight, he
gives birth to his own names . . .

The wise see in their heart, in their spirit, the bird anointed . . .
The poets see him inside the ocean; the sages seek the footprints
of his rays.[12]

In the first verse of this excerpt from the Rig Veda we find the word
eagle being used as a metaphor for the sunbird. The symbol of the eagle
is also found in Hebrew scripture where it becomes a vehicle for spiritual
ascension, as in the book of Exodus when God says to the Israelites, "I bore
you up on eagle's wings and brought you to myself."[13]

What is most odd about the ancient Vedic text however, is the phrase
"Womb of Yama." Womb is something we associate with birth. How is it
that the Hindu god of death could have a womb? The answer I give to this
question is that death in the Vedas is not viewed as an end but as a means of
renewal, just as the leaves die in the fall only to nourish the soil in preparation
for the rebirth of spring. It is birth, not life, that is the opposite of death.
Life is common to both.

Beyond the symbol of the eagle, the image of the sunbird is also implied
in chapter 4 of the Hebrew book of Malachi, which reads, "The sun of
righteousness shall rise with healing in its wings."[14, *]

I mentioned earlier how the phoenix myth may have helped explain
to ancient indigenous people how fire came to earth. The Gospel of Luke
depicts Jesus as a bringer of fire when it quotes him as saying, "I came to
cast fire upon the earth."[15] After Christ's death and resurrection, the Holy
Spirit descended upon the apostles at Pentecost as tongues of fire. Here we
have a remarkable merger of myth and history. For the Christ figure in the
gospels is the sunbird given a human form, a person in whom myth and
history are united. Like the phoenix, he dies, resurrects, and ascends back
to heaven—a testimony to the regenerative nature of life and the potential
we all possess to rise out of our ignorance and live in the light of our higher,
moral, spiritual nature.

---

*   In this passage from Malachi, "wings" is sometimes translated as "rays," as if the rays
of the rising sun are its wings.

The Sustainability Paradigm

The prevailing model for interdisciplinary studies in the 1960s and '70s was known as general systems theory. As a systems theorist, Buchminster Fuller saw the universe as a regenerative system, able to perpetually renew itself. Practically speaking, we see this in the changing of the seasons and in ecosystems as they recover from natural disasters. In 1988, a great forest fire struck Yellowstone National Park. There was much controversy over the policy of the National Park Service to simply allow the park to burn. Ecologists saw the fire as a necessary part of the forest life cycle. They were right. Eventually, from the ashes of this disaster emerged a regenerated and dynamic ecosystem.

We further see this renewal in our own lives as we cope with and strive to overcome personal disappointments and tragedy. Actor Christopher Reeves may have played Superman in the popular movie series, but his true strength was revealed in his efforts to transform his life after his life-changing accident that left him paralyzed from the neck down. Tirelessly he lobbied for embryonic stem cell research which could result in therapies that regenerate human nerve cells and allow victims of paralysis to regain their mobility.

The realization that fossil fuels and other industrial-age resources are rapidly being depleted has contributed to the rise of what is being called the sustainability paradigm. Sustainability requires us to cooperate with the regenerative nature of the earth's ecosystem by shifting our reliance from nonrenewable fossil fuels to "green" renewable resources. It also demands that we apply agricultural practices that rejuvenate the soil, increase local crop diversity, and deter further destruction of the earth's life-giving rain forests.

In contrast, the Jewish and Christian traditions hold on to a familiar verse in the book of Genesis where God commands Adam and Eve to "be fruitful and multiply, and fill the earth and subdue it, and have dominion over every living thing that moves upon the Earth."[16] Allied with the capitalist economic system, this anthropocentric teaching, which I refer to as the dominion paradigm, tempts us into believing we are superior to, and masters of, the natural world. The human species has been remarkably successful at subduing the earth. Genetic engineering, splicing and replacing DNA, cloning mammals, and manipulating the atomic and subatomic building blocks of matter are all technologies now available to us. One can easily say, given these achievements and our prolific population growth, that humans have fulfilled the Genesis commandment.

The dominion paradigm has led to careless exploitation as we rape the earth of its resources and risk destroying the very life-support systems on which civilization depends. It is a problem of the human condition illustrated by a model known as the *tragedy of commons*.

When people share a common resource, there is a tendency to exploit that resource to the extent that it becomes unusable. As Barash and Webel describe it, "Individuals—each seeking to gain personal benefit—find themselves engaging in behavior that is to the disadvantage of everyone."[17] Imagine several sheep ranchers who have their own land but also have access to a "commons," or acreage of land that is shared by the community and on which their sheep also can graze. If each rancher grazes his flock on the commons in moderation, the commons will replenish itself yearly, and they will be able to sustain the land for their sheep. However, the human tendency is for the ranchers to exploit the commons to save their own land, resulting in the destruction of the public acreage.[18]

Such exploitive behavior led to the environmental problems in the United States on Tangier Island. In the early 1960s, it was discovered that watermen in the Chesapeake Bay who were living on Tangier Island were overfishing the waters. Environmental scientists affiliated with the Chesapeake Bay Foundation (CBF) began asking that limits be placed on the number of crabs and oysters harvested by the watermen to insure the seafood population would be sustained and the bay's health restored. The tendency for the watermen, however, was to pollute the bay and exploit the resource to benefit their own livelihood—a practice which, if not restrained, would negatively impact the success of the fishery.[19]

We now have a comparable problem with respect to the earth's atmosphere and the emission of greenhouse gases by industrialized nations. A treaty to curb greenhouse gas emissions will protect the environment and give humanity a sustainable future. It could slow the rise in ocean levels, ease the shift in ocean currents, and temper extreme weather patterns predicted by climate change. Such a treaty calls for nations to exercise restraint in polluting the earth's atmosphere, which is the common resource. Unfortunately, humanity's record in exercising such restraint is not good and hence the phrase "tragedy of commons."

An important factor in avoiding the tragedy of commons appears to be the sense of ownership. In the first illustration above, the sheep ranchers exploit the commons but preserve the land they own. The problem is, people do not see themselves as owning the earth's atmosphere. Is it possible for human beings to care for the earth's atmosphere and its resources as if it belonged to them? Can we instill in people a sense of collective ownership toward the environment and toward planet earth as a living system? While shared ownership may fly in the face of economic motivations in a capitalist system, a religious covenant adopted by the Chesapeake Bay watermen suggests that a collective effort to preserve the environment can succeed.

In 1997, Susan Drake-Emmerich, then a doctoral student at the University of Wisconsin, went to Tangier Island in an effort to mediate the dispute that had arisen between environmental scientists and the Chesapeake Bay watermen. The community in which the fishermen and their families lived was predominately evangelical Christian. In 1995, it had experienced a spiritual revival. Emmerich believed a faith-based approach might provide a resolution to the conflict.

At a church meeting, Emmerich presented the fishermen with biblical passages that instructed believers to respect their neighbors, obey civil authority, and be good stewards of the earth. The result was a community covenant that improved relations between the watermen and environmental scientists and helped insure that limits would be observed on the yearly harvest in terms of the number of crabs caught and their size.[20]

While religion has long been used to justify humanity's dominion over the earth's resources, the experience on Tangier Island demonstrates that religious traditions also can instill a sense of collective ownership and stewardship that promotes sustainability. The effects of global warming could be potentially devastating. Our ability to apply religion as a moral anchor to counter the environmental exploitation predicted by the tragedy of commons may determine whether our civilization can continue to flourish.

The Current Mass Extinction

The annual April celebration of Earth Day in the United States inevitably calls attention to the damage humans continue to inflict on their planetary home. The disastrous oil spill in the Gulf of Mexico in the spring and summer of 2010 should arouse in everyone a great sense of urgency as well as outrage. In a world that is losing its rain forests, where our polluted oceans are losing the ability to sustain fish populations and where glaciers are melting at unprecedented rates, it is vital that we reverse the environmental degradation humanity has caused over the past 150 years.

It is even more troubling to learn of the number of species being threatened with extinction. The majority of biologists now are saying that the earth is undergoing the greatest mass extinction since the time of the dinosaurs.

In the mid-1990s, Harvard naturalist Edward O. Wilson began estimating that thirty thousand species a year were becoming extinct.[21] This is between one hundred and one thousand times greater than what is considered by biologists to be the "background extinction rate."[22] According to the Evolution Library, "The past 400 years have seen 89 mammalian extinctions, almost 45 times the predicted rate."[23] Researchers estimate that if the current rate continues, half the land animals will be extinct by 2100. The cause is no longer natural disasters but human activity in the form of pollution, habitat destruction, climate change, depletion of water resources, and the introduction of invasive species.[24]

In the broader sense, the environmental degradation that leads to species extinction is a violation of the principle of ahimsa or nonviolence. Exhibiting reverence for life must include respect for the survival of nonhuman life-forms as well. It has become a moral imperative for our own survival that we maintain the interdependent web of life of which we are a part and on which we must depend.

Reversing the trend toward environmental exploitation and degradation demands that individuals, communities, and nations commit themselves to the sustainability paradigm, intelligently conserving and managing the earth's resources. We must aggressively accelerate our research and development of solar, wind, hydrogen fuel cell, geothermal, and fusion nuclear technologies to power our civilization. The Malthusian catastrophe predicted by Paul Ehrlich did not take place in the 1980s, and it need not occur today if we launch a green energy revolution with the same intensity that fueled the high-tech revolution during the latter half of the twentieth century.

The Challenge for the Twenty-First Century

A future without war: is it really possible? Given humanity's violent legacy, it is easy for us to become swallowed up in cynicism and resign ourselves to a doomsday scenario. We must keep in mind, however, that our worldview is expanding by leaps and bounds. The Apollo astronauts gave us the first photographs of the earth as an isolated sphere in the vacuum of space. Huge advances in science and technology, and the relatively recent increase in multicultural awareness, virtually force us to see the world in global terms. There are now numerous opportunities available for people the world over to benefit from cultural diversity and acquire a genuine appreciation for the precious oasis of life our planet has evolved to be. But science, technology, and awareness are not enough.

For humanity to evolve into a nonviolent race, we must continue to develop local, national, and international systems of governance that allow injustice to be exposed, addressed, and remedied before violence is perceived as the only option. This calls for responsive social and political systems that guarantee freedom of speech, religion, public assembly, and the right to redress grievances within organizations and within government.

A responsive sociopolitical system also requires a free and responsible news media.* Certainly, Mahatma Gandhi, Alice Paul, Martin Luther King Jr., Cesar Chavez, Nelson Mandela, the current Dalai Lama, and other renowned nonviolent leaders could not have gained public support without a means to inform large and influential sectors of society. With the advent of cell phones, the Internet and social networking websites, the opportunities for exposing oppression and organizing mass protests are unprecedented. This is a great leap forward in the struggle to expose injustice.

As we saw in chapter 4, history shows that nonviolence can be effective, but the majority of successful efforts have occurred domestically within a sovereign nation's borders. The twenty-first-century challenge will be to promote peace education worldwide and apply nonviolent strategies skillfully to settle international disputes. The global economy may, in fact, facilitate grassroots efforts to apply economic pressure across international borders, much like the worldwide boycott of California grapes helped empower the United Farm Workers movement in the 1960's.

It is a mistake, however, to think that a nonviolent world will be a world without conflict. Ralph Waldo Emerson's observation that polarity is present in nature is true for human nature as well. Conflict, therefore, is inherent to life. It is how we deal with conflict that is the issue. We can meet it with anger and hostility or view it as a challenge and an opportunity for civil discourse and constructive change. Local, regional, and national leaders must

---

* Nonviolence, however, does not require a capitalist economic system. There is plenty of evidence that capitalism, left unregulated, actually propagates injustice. Nor must we be too quick to conclude that democracy is the answer. Democracy can only thrive in countries where there are safeguards against corruption and there exists a reasonably educated, literate public. While Western leaders may preach democracy and push for democratic reforms, we must remember that for over a century, the United States propagated a culture that denied equal rights to women and people of color. Let us not forget the words of Winston Churchill: "Indeed, it has been said that democracy is the worst form of government except for all those other forms that have been tried from time to time."

provide opportunities for citizens to vent their frustrations so injustice can be identified and addressed at an early stage. The political process of partisan debate and wrangling is to be expected both nationally and internationally in a nonviolent world, but the discourse must be civil and truthful if it is to be respected. We must master the art of fighting against both our internal anger and our external rivals in honorable, nonviolent ways.

In his seminal treatise the *Yoga Sutras*, the Indian sage Patanjali (ca. 250 BCE) lists ten principles to live by. Often considered the Hindu equivalent to the Ten Commandments, the first five principles, considered restraints, consist of nonviolence (ahimsa), not bearing false witness (truthfulness), not stealing, sexual abstinence, and not coveting (nonattachment). These are followed by five observances, these being purification, contentment, discipline, study of the scriptures, and surrender to the Lord.

In Hinduism, the concept of "Lord" may refer to any one of many representations of deity. Yoga philosophy, however, as expounded in the Bhagavad Gita, conceives of Lord as the "Supreme Self" or "Highest Spirit,"[25] which is first experienced as Atman, then through enlightenment, is realized to be Brahman. This Divinity, this divine image in which we are created, is the source of all true wisdom. It is the great treasure available to all, but it is hidden where we least expect it—within us.* It is closer than the eye, so it cannot be seen, and closer than the "I" (ego), so it cannot be possessed. Beyond the intellect and beyond the ego, the only way to discover it is to surrender, to offer oneself in sacrifice to it.

This observance of surrender can be applied both individually and collectively. Individually, it requires letting go of the ego and the desire to control, living simply, and placing others first. On the deepest interior level, it means allowing the mind, through meditation and reflective prayer, to slip into the experience of its infinite source. Collectively, it speaks to the need for humanity to free itself from the divisive and self-centered conceptions of race, ethnicity, gender roles, class hierarchy, and nationalism.

---

* The treasure metaphor is found in both Hindu and Christian scripture. From the Chandogya Upanishad: "As one, not knowing that a golden treasure lies buried beneath his feet, can walk over it again and again, yet never find it, so all beings live every moment in the city of Brahman, yet never find him, because of the veil of illusion by which he is concealed" (Prabhavananda 1948, 75). And from the Gospel of Matthew: "The Kingdom of Heaven is like a treasure buried in a field which a man found and covered up; then in his joy, he goes and sells all that he has, and buys that field" (Matt. 13:44).

In both domestic affairs and international relations, emphasis must now shift from peace*making* after a violent conflict has erupted, to peace-*building* before violence begins. Deterrence must be sought through building cooperative relationships between people and nations rather than relying so heavily on negative repercussions such as economic sanctions and the threat of military retaliation. In addition to honoring the separation of church and state, American politicians should remove religious language from their political rhetoric. Social justice activists must seek out and expose psychological and structural violence and continue to be advocates for human rights. Moderate religious voices must be given ample opportunity to be heard, and governments must be responsive to and address inequities when and wherever they arise. Peace education and conflict resolution skills must be a requirement in school curricula. Clergy, educators, and high school students must become literate in the language of symbolism and metaphor found in myth and religious scripture, and sustainability and renewable energy must become the design and environmental ethic that is applied uniformly around the globe.

Up until the twentieth century, wars were regional. They could occur without worldwide repercussions and did not threaten humanity as a whole with widespread environmental destruction. But the sophistication and power of modern weaponry, the density of the world population, and the economic and cultural interdependence of our world has changed the human family forever. Wars can no longer be "just," and their consequences can potentially disable the interdependent global economy, the environment, and the agricultural support systems necessary to sustain human life.

It is sobering to think that in the twenty-first century, humans could become threatened with extinction. The cause? Our own shortsighted anthropocentric exploitation of the earth. God may provide each of us with victory over death, but our survival as a human family is up to us. How long will we continue to delude ourselves into believing we are masters of the natural world? How long will we wage wars over land some see as God-given and holy while in our ignorance we fail to treasure the sacred home in the sterile vacuum of space that the earth truly is? Let us first be humbled by the overwhelming power of nature at work in the universe and cultivate a reverent awe and respect for the natural forces that could, at any moment, terminate our existence in this world.

We must also remember that life is regenerative. If humans do become extinct, life will go on. The evolutionary process will undoubtedly replace us with some new species that will rise out of our ashes, as millions of years ago mammals took advantage of the niche that opened when the dinosaurs breathed their last. Perhaps the new species that inherits the earth will have awakened to a higher intelligence so as to be living "with the license of a higher order of beings."[26] For them, night will be as day as they will know the Source of Becoming and the inner light from which epiphanies are born. Having cast aside their selfish, defensive natures, they will walk upright in integrity as well as in stature. They will lead, not by political will, but by the strength of their virtue, the power of their compassion, and the depth of their insights, and they will surrender to the Divine Benefactor presiding within us, rather than seek the surrender of others.

Appendix 1

International Interfaith Organizations

The United Religions Initiative (URI)

Headquarters: San Francisco, California (USA)
www.uri.org
415-561-2300

The United Religions Initiative is a growing global community dedicated to promoting enduring, daily interfaith cooperation, ending religiously motivated violence and creating cultures of peace, justice, and healing for the earth and all living beings.

Working across continents, people from different religions, spiritual expressions, and indigenous traditions are creating unprecedented levels of enduring global cooperation. People's hopes are rising with visions of a better world. It is a world where the values and teachings of the great wisdom traditions guide people's service, where people respect one another's beliefs, and where the resourcefulness and passion of people working together bring healing and a more hopeful future to the earth community. The United Religions Initiative, in time, aspires to have the visibility of the United Nations.

International Interfaith Initiative (III)

Headquarters: Indianapolis, Indiana (USA)
www.internationalinterfaith.org
317-466-0114

The International Interfaith Initiative (III) is designed to foster interfaith cooperation to strengthen civil society. The organization engages in community service projects, convenes conferences, organizes events, conducts original research, educates and informs policymakers, and celebrates diversity through service, interfaith dialogue, and the appreciation of art, music, literature, and cuisine.

The International Interfaith Initiative is based out of the Peace Learning Center in Indianapolis, Indiana (USA), and operates in collaboration with the Indiana University School of Education, the Sagamore Institute for Policy Research, and the Max Kade German-American Center—all working toward the realization of creating an authentic and effective network that inspires, facilitates, and initiates interfaith/intercultural educational service activities.

The International Interfaith Initiative strives to foster collaboration between local, national, and international religious and civic organizations. It recognizes that inter-religious cooperation is vital to successfully combat the chronic issues that plague humankind.

Parliament of World Religions

Headquarters: Chicago, Illinois (USA); Docklands, Victoria
(Australia)
www.parliamentofreligions.org
312-629-2990 (USA)
1300 852 156 or +61 3 8622 4809 (Australia)

Every five years, the Parliament of World Religions sponsors an outstanding international interfaith conference. The Parliament's website makes available articles, videos, and other resource materials and also features a blog. In addition, there is a listing of yearly regional events.

Lakeshore Interfaith Institute

Headquarters: Ganges, Michigan (USA)
www.motherstrust.org
269-543-3951

The Lakeshore Interfaith Institute is an outreach program of Mother's Trust/Mother's Place, Ramakrishna Sarada Ashram, a 501(c)3, a religious order, and an interfaith community. The institute is dedicated to interfaith study and dialogue as one of the many ways to promote understanding and compassionate forgiveness between the world's great wisdom traditions. The sustainability of the earth, compassionate service, and the healing of all living beings are also part of the institute's mission.

Nine-month certification programs are offered in interfaith study and interfaith ministry leading to ordination. Lectures are held every Saturday from April to December, and interfaith worship and dialogue are held on Sundays.

All-Faiths Seminary International

Headquarters: New York, New York (USA
www.allfaithseminary.org
212-866-3795

A seminary based in New York City offering nine-month programs in interfaith ministry as well as advanced degrees. Classes are frequently coordinated with events held at the Lakeshore Interfaith Institute. Correspondence options are available, but participants must attend retreats to qualify for ordination.

Interfaith Alliance

Headquarters: New York, New York; Washington DC
www.interfaithalliance.org
800-510-0969

An organization devoted to protecting religious freedom and diversity in American society. The Interfaith Alliance speaks on behalf of religious minorities particularly when politicians diminish the importance of lesser-known traditions or try to bring the religion of the majority into the political arena. It seeks to maintain appropriate boundaries between government and religion and stands ready to challenge religious extremism.

North American Interfaith Network

www.nain.org

The purpose of the North American Interfaith Network (NAIN) is to serve as a link between interfaith organizations in North America. The

NAIN website lists resource materials such as interfaith videos, books, website links, and journals. Member organizations are required to pay dues on an annual basis.

Converging Streams Interfaith Ministry

Headquarters: Lifeworks Center, Muncie, Indiana (USA)
www.convergingstreams.org
765-286-8221

Converging Streams offers a structured approach to interfaith dialogue and worship. Its prominent symbol is the Möbius strip. The organization makes available resources for interfaith worship and discussion, as well as interfaith radio programs. It also holds interfaith psalm-writing workshops. Radio broadcasts of *Converging Streams: Interfaith Fellowship in our Modern World,* are available for download.

Appendix 2

Meditation and the Gandharva Tradition

Meditation is an effective way to heighten mental clarity, alleviate stress, and achieve a tranquil state of quiet inner reflection. A technique derived from the Gandharva musical tradition in India allows practitioners to bring the harmony underlying creation to the surface of life where it can be experienced and lived in a practical way.

Think of the mind as a pond of water, which, when left undisturbed, presents us with a clear picture of the images reflecting off its surface. It is the mind's nature to reflect what we take in through the senses, but tension and fatigue in daily life create "waves" on the surface of the mind, causing it to present us with a convoluted image, distorting our perception of reality. *Gandharva Meditation* is a technique that enables us to restore the mind to its natural condition of tranquility so it can yield a truer reflection of reality.

During Gandharva Meditation, the silence at the depths of the mind comes to the foreground of our experience while mental activity settles into the background and can even subside altogether. It is a psycho-physiological experience, simultaneously a condition of heightened awareness and deep relaxation. The technique does not involve forced concentration, and it is quite easy to learn.

This form of meditation is not a mood, nor is it a form of self-hypnosis or autosuggestion. It is a state of consciousness as tangible and as real as waking, sleeping, or dreaming—a means of experiencing the ground of *being* that lies at the depths of our consciousness.

One first learns how to establish the proper conditions in the physiology for the body's metabolism to reduce significantly through the use of an ancient form of East Indian music. Then a technique is used that allows a person to cooperate with the mind's natural tendency to settle into to a quiet state of non-desire. This experience of inner pleasantness cultures in the individual the state of attunement characterized by a heightened state of cooperation between the voluntary and involuntary nervous systems. It is a procedure that is practiced twice a day and takes approximately twenty minutes. For more information, contact:

Lifeworks Center
2417 West Jackson Street
Muncie, Indiana 47304
765-286-8221

Appendix 3

The Growth of Human Consciousness: The Nine Pivotal Awakenings

1. 0-1 years of age:* Awakening to "self-awareness";
   Awareness of the difference between self and object of perception.
2. 1-2 years of age: Awakening to right and wrong, good and bad;
   Awareness of social rules and expectations.
3. 2-5 years of age: Awakening to body as self;
   Awareness of embarrassment and being naked, awareness of death.
4. 5-12 years of age: Awakening of the intellect;
   Increased ability to think logically.
5. 12-18 years of age: Puberty and the awakening of sexuality;
   Awareness of sexual differences and the desire for intimacy.
   Motivated by one's physical needs and the needs of the ego.
6. 18-25 years of age: Awakening to the higher spiritual "Self";
   Awareness of an identity independent of physical self and ego.
   Recognition of moral dilemmas and imperfection as part of the human condition.
7. 25-35 years of age: Awareness of higher "Self" permanently established;
   Actions motivated by the needs of environment, the needs of others, and the "greater good." The "higher Self" is recognized as eternal, conquering the fear of death.

---

* The ages given here are approximate, and the awakening experiences can overlap one another.

8.   35-50 years of age: Awareness of subtle values revealed through ongoing realizations;
      Perceiving life and meaning in terms of symbolism, metaphor, and myth. One is now increasingly able to follow one's "inner light."
9.   50-100 years of age: Awakening to "Oneness" and the interconnectedness of life;
      Realization that the higher "Self" is the "Self of all beings." Experiencing both the joy and pain of others as one's own.

Symbols for awakening are as follows:

(1) caterpillar becoming a butterfly and
(2) second birth.

Endnotes

Introduction

1. Mahabharata 5:1517.
2. Udana-Varga 5.18.
3. Talmud, Shabbat 31a.
4. Matthew 7:12.
5. Luke 10:30-35.
6. Luke 10:29.
7. Purvis, *The Samaritan Pentateuch and the Origin of the Samaritan Sect,* 4-5.
8. Barash and Webel, *Peace and Conflict Studies,* 120-122.
9. *Seville Statement on Violence,* 12.
10. *Ibid.,* 30.
11. Hunt, *The Compassionate Beast,* 11-13.
12. Matthew 13:10-16.
13. Matthew 9:18-25
14. Pagels, *The Gnostic Gospels,* xxi-xxiv.
15. Durant, *The Story of Civilization III,* 654-655.
16. Pagels, *The Gnostic Gospels,*145.
17. Matthew 5:14-15.
18. Ryan, "Recruiting for Terror," *Frontpage Magazine.*
19. Gora, "Ball State's Critics Ignore Facts, Policies." *The Star Press,* 5A.
20. Editorial, *Journal Gazette,* Dec. 27, 2004; Editorial, *The Star Press,* Feb. 7, 2005.
21. Glazov, Jamie. "Making Peace With David Horowitz." *FrontPageMagazine. com.*
22. Wink, *The Powers That Be,* 168-172.

Chapter 1

1. Matthew 24:30.
2. I Thessalonians: 4:16, 17.
3. Matthew 24:29.
4. Cleary, *The Essential Koran,* 133.
5. Sells, *Approaching the Qur'an,* 52.
6. Singh, *Hinduism,* 55.
7. Revelation 19:11-15.
8. Gaer, *What the Great Religions Believe,* 222.
9. Davies, *The First Christian,* 120-121; Allegro, *The Dead Sea Scrolls and the Christian Myth,* 111.
10. Gaer, *What the Great Religions Believe,* 227.
11. John 3:19-20.
12. Numbers, ch. 31-34.
13. Will, *Kerry Was Right,* 6A.
14. Boyer, *When Time Shall Be No More,* 145.
15. II Thessalonians. 2:3-12.
16. Bush, G. H. W., *Televised address to congress.*
17. *CNN Late Addition with Wolf Blitzer* (transcript), October 24, 2004.
18. Heyking, *Iran's President and the Politics of the Twelfth Iman,* 1-2.
19. Prabhavananda & Manchester, *The Upanishads,* xii.
20. Romans 13:12.
21. Romans 7:14-23.
22. Ephesians 6:14-17.
23. Luke 6:27 and 35.
24. Romans 12:21.
25. Matthew 11:12.
26. Barash & Webel, *Peace and Conflict Studies,* 411.
27. Rahman, "The Real Meaning of Jihad." *The Star Press,* 20.
28. Armstrong, *The Battle for God,* 243.
29. Qur'an, surah 2:62.
30. Shanks, "Rediscovering the Kathisma where Mary Rested." *Biblical Archaeology Review,* 50-51.
31. Numbers 31:17-18.
32. Deuteronomy 7:2.
33. Qur'an, surah 8:12.
34. Qur'an, surah 4:89.
35. Qur'an, surah 4:90.

36. Swing, *The Coming United Religions,* 46.
37. Qur'an, surah 2:26.
38. Qur'an, surah 2:256.
39. Malachi 4:1.
40. Luke 12:49.
41. Isaiah 25: 7.
42. 2nd Corinthians 3:14, 15.
43. 2nd Corinthians 3:16, 18.
44. Nikhilananda, *The Upanishads,* Vol. I, 53.
45. Matthew 24:40-42.
46. Nikhilananda, *The Upanishads,* Vol. I, 297-300.
47. Tapasananda: *The Kingdon of Heaven is Within You,* 10.
48. Luke 17:21.
49. Matthew 24:27.
50. Revelation 21:2.
51. Rajagopalachari, *Mahabharata,* 302.
52. Revelation 21:2.
53. 2nd Corinthians 3:16.
54. 1st Corinthians 15: 51-52.
55. 1st Corinthians 13:12.

Chapter 2

1. Feng & English, trans. *Tao Te Ching,* ch. 22,
2. Matthew 10:39.
3. Goldwater 1964 campaign flyer - www.4president.org/brochures/goldwater1964brochure.htm
4. www.malcolm-x.org/quotes.htm
5. Wolpert, *Gandhi's Passion,* 113-114.
6. Gilbert, *Winston S. Churchill,* vol 4, part 3, 1644-45.
7. Herman, *Gandhi and Churchill,* 507.
8. Thoreau, *Walden* (with an introduction and annotations by Bill McKibben), 105-106.
9. Hanh, *Living Buddha, Living Christ,* 10.
10. Merton, *Spiritual Direction and Meditation,* 52-54.
11. Prabhavananda & Manchester, *The Upanishads,* 28-29.
12. Hanh, *Living Buddha, Living Christ,* 76.
13. Müeller, *The Dhammapada,* Ch. 21: verses 296-301; 80.
14. Prabhavananda & Manchester, *The Upanishads,* 20.

15. Ephesians, 5:14.
16. Mark 13:35, 36.
17. Nagler, *The Search for a Nonviolent Future,* 50.
18. Matthew 5:10.
19. Malachi 3:2-3.
20. Emerson, *Essays,* 22.
21. Herman, *Gandhi and Churchill,* 178.
22. Rajagopalachari, *Mahabharata,* 318, 321.
23. Matthew 2: 1-2.
24. Matthew 2: 16-18.
25. Wolpert, *Gandhi's Passion,* 101.
26. Herman, *Gandhi and Churchill,* 258.
27. Ibid., 255-257.
28. Zinn, *The Power of Nonviolence,* 4.

Chapter 3

1. Kendall, "Pope Paul VI's Aphorism—'If You Want Peace Work for Justice'—and the Nobel Prize WInners," 39.
2. Matthew, 7:3-5.
3. John 14:27.
4. Deutsch, (trans.), *The Bhagavad Gita,* 45-46.
5. Galtung, "Twenty Years of Peace Research: Ten Challenges and Responses." *Journal of Peace Research,* vol. 22, 414-431.
6. Barash & Webel, *Peace and Conflict Studies,* 6.
7. Unitarian Universalist Association of Congregations, *Creating Peace: Statement of Conscience.*
8. Rajagopalachari, *Mahabharata,* 302.
9. Galtung, "Twenty Years of Peace Research: Ten Challenges and Responses," 414-431.
10. Barash & Webel, *Peace and Conflict Studies,* 7.
11. Jezer; Cooney, and Michalowski, eds., *The Power of the People,* 127.
12. Merton, *The Nonviolent Alternative,* 224.
13. www.historylearningsite.co.uk/civilian_casualties_of_world_war.htm
14. www.afsc.org/iraq
15. Emerson, *Essays,* 61-64.
16. Galatians 6:7.
17. Ecclesiastes 1:4-7.
18. King, *Public Address,* Montgomery, Alabama, March 25, 1965.

Chapter 4

1. Jezer; Cooney, and Michalowski, eds., *The Power of the People*, 15-17.
2. Ibid., 15-17.
3. Ibid., 17.
4. Ibid., 24-28.
5. Ibid., 33.
6. Ballou, Christian Non-Restance, 2-21.
7. Gandhi, *The Way to God*, 38.
8. Nagler, *The Search for a Nonviolent Future*, 44, 45.
9. Deutsch, trans., *The Bhagavad Gita*, 67.
10. Barash & Webel, *Peace and Conflict Studies*, 522.
11. Nagler, *The Search for a Nonviolent Future*, 46.
12. Rolland, *Mahatma Gandhi*, 52-53.
13. Nagler, *The Search for a Nonviolent Future*, 47.
14. Wink, *The Powers that Be*, 119.
15. Herman, *Gandhi and Churchill*, 177.
16. Matthew 5:38-39.
17. Wink, *The Powers that Be*, 101-103.
18. Psalm 23:5.
19. Stengel, *Mandela's Way*, 12-15.
20. Mandela, *Inaugural Address*, May 14, 1994.
21. Deutsch, trans., *The Bhagavad Gita*, Ch. 2 vs. 20 and 23.
22. Ibid., ch. 2 vs. 31and 33.
23. Ibid., ch. 2 vs. 34 and 37.
24. Ibid., ch. 3 vs. 36 and 43.
25. Ibid., ch. 17 vs. 14 and 16.
26. Yogi, *The Bhagavad Gita*, 27.
27. Rajagopalachari, *Mahabharata*, 34.
28. Thomas, *So Long Until Tomorrow*, 136.
29. Ibid., 166-167.
30. Wink, *The Powers that Be*, 168-172.
31. Jezer; Cooney, and Michalowski, eds., *The Power of the People*, 62-71.
32. Ibid., 176-181.
33. Ibid., 224-239.
34. Barash and Webel, *Peace and Conflict Studies*, 104-105.
35. Donovan, *Poland: Solidarity—The Trade Union That Changed the World*.
36. Ruchames, ed., *Racial Thought in America*, 263-288.
37. Jezer; Cooney, and Michalowski, eds., *The Power of the People*, 76-81.

38. Ibid.,182.
39. LaCapra, *Critique on Violence,* Public address.

Chapter 5

1. Feng & English, trans., *Tao Te Ching.* Introduction.
2. Ibid., ch. 1.
3. Ibid., ch. 6.
4. Ibid., ch. 22.
5. Ibid., ch. 25.
6. Ibid., ch. 52.
7. Luke 14:11.
8. Matthew. 19:30.
9. Mark 10:15.
10. Feng & English, trans., *Tao Te Ching,* ch. 28.
11. Ibid., ch. 4.
12. Ibid., ch. 11.
13. Pagels, *Beyond Belief,* 259.
14. Feng & English, trans., *Tao Te Ching,* ch.28.
15. *History of Kung-Fu,* www.talkkungfu.co.uk/guides/history_of_kung_fu.html.
16. Feng & English, trans., *Tao Te Ching,* ch.78.
17. Ibid., ch. 43.
18. Ibid., ch. 76.
19. Ibid., ch. 31.
20. Ibid., ch. 31.
21. Ibid., ch. 68.
22. Ibid., ch. 73.
23. Ibid., ch. 59.
24. Ibid., ch. 64.
25. *Interview with Robert Bly,* www.pbs.org/kued/nosafeplace/interv/bly.html.
26. *The Mankind Project,* www.mkp.org.

Chapter 6

1. Wink, *The Powers that Be,* 45.
2. Ibid., 42-56.
3. Ibid., 42.

4. Ibid., 45.
5. Ibid., 45, 46.
6. Exodus 14:15-29.
7. Exodus 4:1-5.
8. Greenwald, *Uncovered: The War on Iraq Transcript,* 31.
9. Ibid., 28.
10. U.S. Senator, *Radio Free Europe, Radio Liberty.* www.rferl.org.
11. Mortenson and Relin, *Three Cups of Tea,* 2006.
12. King, *Stride Toward Freedom: The Montgomery Circle,* 13-16.
13. Barash and Webel, *Peace and Conflict Studies,* 125-126.
14. Ibid., 125-126.
15. McCullough, *Beyond Revenge,* 81-82.
16. Herman, *Gandhi and Churchill,* 555-556.
17. *Public attitudes towards the war in Iraq: 2003-2008,* Pew Research Center, 2008.
18. Matthew 6:19.

Chapter 7

1. *The United Nations Declaration of Human Rights.*
2. Fuller, *Operating Manual for Spaceship Earth,* 89.
3. Ibid., 123.
4. Ibid., 90.
5. Ibid., 65.
6. Thoreau, *Walden* (with an introduction and annotations by Bill McKibben), 291.
7. Watts, *Myth and Ritual in Christianity,* 147.
8. Thoreau, *Walden* (with an introduction and annotations by Bill McKibben), 311-312.
9. Schrödinger, *What is Life,* 67-75.
10. John 10:10b
11. Thoreau, *Walden* (with an introduction and annotations by Bill McKibben), 85.
12. O'Flaherty, trans., *Rig Veda,* 190-193.
13. Exodus 19:4
14. Malachi 4: 2.
15. Luke 12:49.
16. Genesis 1:28.
17. Barash and Webel, *Peace and Conflict Studies,* 464.

18. Ibid., 463.

19. Emmerich and Pohorski, *Between Heaven and Earth*.

20. Ibid.

21. Wilson, *The Diversity of Life*.

22. Connor, *Earth Faces 'Catastrophic Loss of Species.'*

23. www.pbs.org/wgbh/evolution/library/03/2/l_032_04.html.

24. www.well.com/user/davidu/extinction.html.

25. Deutsch, trans., *The Bhagavad Gita*, ch. 15 vs. 17.

26. Thoreau, *Walden* (with an introduction and annotations by Bill McKibben), 303.

Bibliography

Ali, Abdullah Yusuf. *The Meaning of the Holy Qur'an,* 11th ed. Beltsville, Md.: Amana Publications, 2004.

Allegro, John. *The Dead Scrolls and the Christian Myth.* Buffalo, N.Y.: Prometheus Books, 1984.

Armstrong, Karen. *The Battle for God.* New York: Alfred A Knopf, 2000.

Ballou, Adin. *Christian Non-Resistance, in All Its Important Bearings, Illustrated and Defended.* London: Charles Gilpin, 1848.

Barash, David P. and Webel, Charles P. *Peace and Conflict Studies.* London: Sage Publications, 2002.

Boyer, Paul. *When Time Shall Be No More: Prophecy and Belief in Modern American Culture.* Cambridge, MA: Harvard University Press, 1992.

Bush, George Herbert Walker. *Televised address to congress,* September 11, 1990.

Cleary, Thomas, trans. *The Essential Koran: The Heart of Islam.* San Francisco: Harper, 1993.

CNN Late Edition with Wolf Blitzer (transcript). transcripts.cnn.com. October 24, 2004.

Conner, Steve. *Earth Faces 'Catastrophic Loss of Species.'* www.commondreams.org/headlines06/0720-08.htm, 2006.

Davies, A. Paul. *The First Christian: A study of St. Paul and Christian Origins.* NewYork: Farrar, Straus and Cudahy, 1957.

Deshpande, M. S., ed. *The Way to God: Selected Writings from Mahatma Gandhi.* Berkley: North Atlantic Books, 2009.

Deutsch, Elliot. trans. *The Bhagavad Gita.* New York: Holt, Reinhart and Winston, 1968.

Donovan, Jeffrey. "Poland: Solidarity—The Trade Union that Changed the World." *Radio Free Europe / Radio Liberty.* www.rferl.org/content/article/1060898.html. August 24, 2005.

Durant, Will. *The Story of Civilization III: Caesar and Christ.* New York: Simon and Schuster, 1944.

Editorial. "No Demonstrated Need for College Rights Bill." *The Star Press.* Muncie, Indiana: Feb. 7, 2005.

Editorial. "Unneeded 'Bill of Rights'." *Journal Gazette.* Fort Wayne, Indiana: December 27, 2004.

Ehrlich, Paul R. *The Population Bomb.* New York: Ballantine Books, 1968.

Emerson, Ralph W. *Essays,* Limited ed. Franklin Center, Pa.: The Franklin Library, 1981.

Emmerich, Susan D. and Pohorski, Jeffrey. *Between Heaven and Earth: The Plight of the Chesapeake Watermen.* Los Angeles: Skunkfilms Inc., 2001.

Feng, Gia-Fu, and English, Jane, trans. *Tao Te Ching,* 25th anniversary ed. New York: Vintage Books, 1997.

Fuller, R. Buckminster. *Operating Manual for Spaceship Earth.* New York: Simon and Schuster, 1969.

Gaer, Joseph. *What the Great Religions Believe.* New York: Dodd, Mead & Company, 1963.

Galtung, Johan. "Twenty Years of Peace Research: Ten Challenges and Responses." *Journal of Peace Research* vol. 22: 414-431, 1985.

Gilbert, Martin. *Winston S. Churchill: Vol. 4, Companion* Documents. parts 1-3. Boston: Houghton Mifflin, 1977.

Glazov, Jamie. "Making Peace With David Horowitz." *FrontPageMagazine.com.* http://97.74.65.51/readArticle.aspx?ARTID=35212, June 15, 2009.

Gora, Jo Ann. "Ball State's Critics Ignore Facts, Policies." *The Star Press,* Muncie, Indiana, December 15, 2004.

Greenwald, Robert. *Uncovered: The War on Iraq Transcript.* www.truthuncovered.com/UNCOVEREDtranscript.pdf, 2004.

Hanh, Thich Nhat. *Living Buddha, Living Christ.* New York: Riverhead Books, 1995.

Helminski, Kabir, trans. *The Rumi Collection.* Boston: Shambala, 2000.

Herman, Arthur. *Gandhi and Churchhill: The Epic Rivalry that Destroyed an Empire and Forged Our Age.* New York: Bantam Dell, 2008.

Heyking, John von. "Iran's President and the Politics of the Twelfth Iman." *Ashbrook Center for Public Affairs.* www.ashbrook.org/publicat/guest/05/vonheyking/twelfthimam.html, 2005.

History of Kung-Fu. www.talkkungfu.co.uk/guides/history_of_kung_fu.html.

Hunt, Morton. *The Compassionate Beast: What Science is Discovering About the Humane Side of Humankind.* New York: William Morrow and Company, Inc.,1990.

Interview with Robert Bly. www.pbs.org/kued/nosafeplace/interv/bly.html.

Jezer, Marty; Cooney, Robert and Michalowski, Helen eds. *The Power of the People: Active Nonviolence in the United States.* Philadelphia: New Society Publishers, 1987.

Kendall, Walter. "Pope Paul VI's Aphorism—'If You Want Peace Work for Justice'—and the Nobel Peace Prize Winners." *The Acorn,* vol. 11 no. 1, fall-winter: 38-55, 2001.

King, Martin Luther. *Stride Toward Freedom: The Montgomery Circle.* New York: Harper & Row, 1958.

LaCapra, Dominick. *Critique on Violence.* (Keynote address delivered at the International Conference on the Humanities), Honolulu, Hawaii, January 5-9, 2003.

Lombardi, Francis G.; Lombardi, Gerald Scott. *Circle Without End: A Sourcebook of American Indian Ethics.* Happy Camp, CA.: Naturegraph, 1982.

McCullough, E. Michael. *Beyond Revenge: The Evolution of the Forgiveness Instinct.* San Francisco: Jossey-Bass, 2008.

Merton, Thomas. *The Nonviolent Alternative.* New York: Farrar, Straus, Giroux, 1971.

Merton, Thomas. *Spiritual Direction and Meditation.* Collegeville, Minnesota: Order of St. Benedict, 1960.

Mortenson, Greg & Relin, David Oliver. *Three Cup of Tea: One Man's Mission to Fight Terrorism and Build Nations... One School at a Time.* New York: Viking Pengun, 2006.

Müeller, Friedrich Max, trans. *The Dhammapada.* Norwood Austrialia: Deodand Publishing, 2002.

Nagler, Michael N. *The Search for a Nonviolent Future: A Promise of Peace for Ourselves, Our Families and Our World.* Navato, Ca.: New World Library, 2004.

Nikhilananda, Swami. *The Upanishads: Katha, Isa, Kena, and Mundaka,* Vol. I. New York: RamaKrishna-Vivekananda Center, 1949.

O'Flaherty, Wendy D. *The Rig Veda: An Anthology.* London: Penguin Books, 1981.

Pagels, Elaine. *Beyond Belief: The Gospel of Thomas.* New York: Bantam Books, 2004.

Pagels, Elaine. *The Gnostic Gospels.* Vintage Books ed. New York: Random House, 1981.

Prabhavananda, Swami, & Manchester, Frederick. *The Upanishads: Breath of the Eternal.* New York: The New American Library, 1948.

Public attitudes towards the war in Iraq: 2003-2008. Pew Research Center Publications. 2008.

Purvis, James D. *The Samaritan Pentateuch and the Origin of the Samaritan Sect.* Cambridge, Ma.: Harvard University Press, 1968.

Rahman, Faiz. "The Real Meaning of Jihad." *The Star Press,* Muncie, Indiana, August 6, 2005.

Rajagopalachari, C. *Mahabharata.* Bombay: Bharatiya Vidya Bhavan, 1990.

Rolland, Romain, Catherine D. Groth, trans. *Mahatma Gandhi.* London: Swarthmore Press, 1924.

Ruchames, Louis ed. *Racial Thought in America: From the Puritans to Abraham Lincoln.* New York: Grosset and Dunlap, 1969.

Ryan, Thomas. "Recruiting for Terror." *Frontpage Magazine.com. http://97.74.65.51/readArticle.aspx?ARTID=10660,* Nov. 8, 2004.

Schrodinger, Erwin. *What is Life: The Physical Aspects of the Living Cell.* Cambridge: Cambridge University Press, 1967.

Sells, Michael, trans. *Approaching the Qur'an: the Early Revelations.* Ashland, Oregon: White Cloud Press, 1999.

Seville Statement on Violence. New York: UNESCO, 1991.

Shanks, Hershel. "Rediscovering the Kathisma where Mary Rested." *Biblical Archaeology Review,* November / December issue, 2006.

Singh, Dharam Vir. *Hinduism: an Introduction.* New Delhi: Shree Baidyanath Ayurved Bhawan Ltd., 1991.

Stengel, Richard. *Mandela's Way: Fifteen Lessons on Life, Love, and Courage.* New York: Crown, 2010.

Subramaniam, Kamala, trans. *Srimad Bhagavatam,* 7th ed. Mumbai: Bharatiya Vidya Bhavan, Kulapati Munshi Marg, 1997.

Swing, William E. *The Coming United Religions.* Grand Rapids: CoNexus Press, 1998.

Tapasananda, Swami. *The Kingdom of Heaven is Within You,* (unpublished manuscript) Ganges, Michigan: Lakeshore Interfaith Institute, 2002.

Thomas, Lowell. *So Long Until Tomorrow: From Quaker Hill to Kathmandu.* New York: William Morrow and Company Inc., 1977.

Thoreau, Henry David. *Walden* (with an introduction and annotations by Bill McKibben). Boston: Beacon Press, 1997.

Unitarian Universalist Association of Congregations. *Creating Peace: Statement of Conscience.* www.uua.org/socialjustice/socialjustice/statements/13394.shtml, 2010.

"U.S. Senator, NED Laud Iran's Green Movement." *Radio Free Europe, Radio Liberty.* www.rferl.org/content/McCain_Remarks__NED__Iran_Opposition_And_US/2069285.html, June 12, 2010.

Watts, Alan W. *Myth and Ritual and Christianity.* Boston: Beacon Press, 1968.

Will, George. "Kerry was right: usual tactics don't work." Syndicated Column, *The Star Press,* Muncie, Indiana, Aug. 16, 2006.

Wilson, Edward O. *The Diversity of Life.* New York: W. W. Norton and Co, 1999.

Wink, Walter. *The Powers that Be: Theology for a New Millennium.* New York: Doubleday, 1998.

Wolpert, Stanley. *Gandhi's Passion: The Life and Legacy of Mahatma Gandhi.* Oxford University Press, 2001.

Wu, John C. H. trans. *Tao Te Ching.* Boston: Shambala Publications, Inc., 1961.

Yogi, Maharishi M. *The Bhagavad Gita, A New Translation and Commentary.* London: International SRM Publications, 1967.

Zinn, Howard. *The Power of Nonviolence: Writings by Advocates of Peace.* Boston: Beacon Press, 2002.

Index

About the Author

George Wolfe is currently the coordinator of outreach programs for the Center for Peace and Conflict Studies at Ball State University where he served as director of peace studies from 2002 to 2006. He is a certified mediator and was trained to conduct interfaith dialogue at All-Faiths Seminary International in New York City where he was ordained an interfaith minister. In 1991, he was awarded an open fellowship from the Eli Lilly Endowment which made possible his first trip to India where he became interested in the nonviolent philosophy of Mahatma Gandhi.

Wolfe received his doctorate in higher education administration from Indiana University. As an educator, he frequently lectures both within and outside the United States on topics related to nonviolence, peace education, academic freedom, and the role of the arts in social activism. He is a member of the advisory council of the Toda Institute for Peace, Policy and Global Research, and has served as a visiting scholar at Limburg Catholic University in Hasselt, Belgium. In the spring of 2007, he presented peace education workshops in the island nation of Saint Lucia by invitation of the Ministry of Education.

Dr. Wolfe is also a classical saxophonist who holds the rank of Professor of Music Performance at Ball State University. He has appeared as a soloist with such ensembles as the Chautauqua Motet Choir, the U.S. Navy Band Brass Quintet, the Saskatoon Symphony, and the Royal Band of the Belgian Air Force. He has also given recitals and master classes throughout the United States, as well as at major conservatories and universities in Europe, Central America, and the Far East.

The Author at Walden Pond

Edwards Brothers,Inc!
Thorofare, NJ 08086
04 March, 2011
BA2011063